Introduction to FINANCIAL SUCCESS

By Carling D. Colbert, Sr.

Freebird Publishers
North Dighton, MA

Freebird Publishers
Box 541, North Dighton, MA 02764
Info@FreebirdPublishers.com
www.FreebirdPublishers.com

Introduction to Financial Success
By Carling D. Colbert, Sr.

ISBN: 978-1-952159-29-9

Printed in the United States of America

DEDICATION

This book is dedicated to my beautiful mother, Betty M. Thomas, who birthed and loved me despite the circumstances. Special thanks to my three gorgeous sisters who have supported me through the years: Alicia, Ennis, and DeChristina. Thanks to the mother of my children who blessed me with the privilege of being the father to four extraordinarily gifted children: Carlee, Carling II, Daniel, and Landen. You four have been a great motivator for me to complete this book. Shout out to all my nieces and nephews who show me love like I am the greatest uncle in the world. I want to thank my aunts, uncles, and all my cousins, who were more like brothers and sisters, for all the support. My family is too large to name everyone, but I want to shout out the Colberts, Hightowers, Thomases, Duggers, Davises, and the Walkers. Finally, to the grandmothers who helped raised me, Beatrice "Nent" Hightower Colbert and Christine "Chris" Thomas: I love you both for the time we had together.

ACKNOWLEDGEMENTS

Shout out to my military buddies, my brothers and sisters, and all the newfound friends and associates who supported me through the completion of this book: Steven Holsey, Antonio Moore, Wesley Eaton, Arthur Martin, Robert Atkinson, and the men of the United States Disciplinary Barracks. I would also like to give a special thanks to my college professors: Angela Consani, my biology professor from Kansas City Kansas Community College, who saw that I was an exceptional young man and believed in me; and Dr. Waller, my English I and II professor, who saw talent in my writing and encouraged me to pursue it.

For all the people who purchased this book, I want to say, "Thanks for the love." Your purchase not only helps me but also helps other incarcerated veterans and low-income personnel through a side project I call Operation HOT GRitS (Helping Our Troops Get Reintegrated to Society). The majority of my proceeds will help people find affordable housing and attain work, so that they too can become financially successful. I deeply thank you all, and once again I would like to shout out my ex-wife for our beautiful children and ten years of marriage. Without any further hesitation, *Let's get to it.*

BACKGROUND

While writing this book I came across an excerpt from Ben Robson's book *Currency Kings* that said something about everyone having a book in them. Well, this is just one of the many I feel I have within me. The information contained in this book is based upon my own personal experiences and those of others, research, and general knowledge. I desire to help you obtain a better understanding of finance so that you too can get on your way to wealth. But before I begin with the good stuff, I would like to give you a little background of how this book came into being.

From a very young age money and I had a love/hate relationship; I loved it when I had it but hated it when there never seemed to be enough in the household, especially when I could not have the things my cousins and other children had. I was always fascinated with money and the accumulation of it. As a child I would iron every wrinkled bill I would get because I liked having my money crisp. I also loved having it in abundance; this was all before I knew the power money held, or rather the power we allow it to hold, and well before I got intimate with the intricacies of money and finance.

I thought I had an understanding of money when I was younger because I saved, but little did I know that saving did not even scratch the surface of the subject with money. Even saving did not really work, because coming from a lower-middle class background as soon as I saw that my stash had gained some commas, I wanted to spend it … and spend it I did, just like that 2 Chainz song.

As soon as I got old enough to go on my own, I joined the military. I got a $20,000 bonus for joining during wartime, and once I got it, I blew it on useless things such as named-brand clothes, partying, and plain old having fun. Initially I blamed it on my upbringing, in that I was sort of sheltered and did not gain an education on money, and the fact that I was young. But the truth is I did it because I was free to do whatever the hell I wanted. I was "grown," plus I did not look at the bigger picture. I had no self-control.

I was used to living paycheck-to-paycheck in my household, so once I got it I spent it thinking that my military check would be enough and that once I did 20 years or more in the military that my pension would hold me. Once again, I was shortsighted in my thinking.

During my eight years in the Army, I squandered hundreds of thousands of dollars on clothes, new cars – on an almost annual basis – alcohol, cigarettes, video games, and partying. This includes paychecks, bonuses, five-figure tax returns, raises, and even the dividend you get for being an Alaskan citizen! Yep, I was one hell a reckless dude with my spending, even after having married at 18, and supporting a wife and six children before the age of 30.

I mean we were Ralph Lauren down to the socks yet struggling to have enough gas in the car at times. I am talking $200 custom POLO shirts with our names embroidered, just so we could impress others. How silly, right? I was a king in a glass castle; I had no assets to speak of – no house, no stocks, and no retirement account(s). I can finally be honest with myself and admit that I was a sorry excuse for a husband and father during that time. And to think, my kids thought we were rich.

It took me losing everything and hitting rock bottom to get my shit together. I mean I lost my career, my family, the "things" I thought brought me happiness, and my pride; this was over seven years ago. Now I am currently making less than $1,500 a year, but I am using what funds I have to build a better future. I save and invest so that I will not have to burden my family once I leave incarceration. I have made plans to start businesses so that I can finally live my best life. One of my top goals is to not have to depend on an employer for my livelihood and that is partly why you are reading this book.

I am not trying to elicit sympathy or brag, I do this because maybe you can learn from my mistakes and make better choices, so that your life is better than it currently is.

There are many purposes for me writing this book. First, I wrote this book to empower you into action. We as people have allowed the news and other media into our minds and most of us accept their propaganda as gospel. In this book I give you what I have deemed to be the most important facts, real, relevant facts, along with any experiences I can offer. Do not just take my word for it, fact-check what I have said in here for yourself.

Everything in this book may not work for everyone, so do not hold that against me. And some things may have changed by the time this hits the press, as technology is constantly evolving.

Secondly, I wrote this to encourage financial success. Only you can define what that looks like for yourself. I only give you the information to be used in whatever manner you see fit.

Third of all, I wrote this book to pass the knowledge I have acquired on to you in as simple a manner as possible. There will be some technical language contained within, but I did my best to make it relatable. However, if you intend on venturing into the areas contained inside this book then it is best to learn the lingo.

Finally, I wrote this book to gain capital I can use to help other incarcerated veterans. Eighty percent of the proceeds earned from the sale of this book will go to help create affordable living arrangements for personnel who may not have a place to go to once they leave military confinement. I am working the details out with a partner willing to help bring this to fruition.

I am not in the position to fully utilize all the knowledge I have acquired or chose to explain in this book, however, that does not stop you from using it. I know for a fact that the areas in this book will work if you take appropriate action. I have spoken and worked with people who are making money at this moment by trading or investing in the markets, as well as structuring real estate deals.

This book is not intended to be just another feel good book; I actually want to make a difference in your life. People claim that it is lonely at the top, but it does not have to be if you follow the information outlined in this book and pass the same knowledge on to others. I have tried with my own family to no avail, but that is another story in itself. I am simply trying to do what my extended family taught me, which is "each one, teach one," so that is what I intend to do. If you are truly ready to change your circumstances, then turn the page and begin your journey into understanding financial success.

CONTENTS

INTRODUCTION

Success in life is about becoming what you want to be. By purchasing this book, I am deducing that you want to become financially successful, you support my cause, or you wanted to see the information I am presenting. Whatever motivated you, thanks for making this transaction.

I grew up wanting to be wealthy but was made to feel like money was evil. People in my socioeconomic class did not truly understand the concept of money. As an adult I now realize that there is nothing wrong with wanting to be financially free, rich, or wealthy. If you too desire this then it only means that you desire a richer, fuller, and more abundant life than what you are currently or constantly enduring.

When I was growing up the assumption was that in order to have riches or wealth you had to be some unscrupulous or greedy person who only cared about money, yet this was and is far from the truth. Yes, there are some people who have attained their status in life by using unsavory methods, and this most likely stems from the "scarcity mentality." But that does not describe everyone who has achieved financial success. In order to achieve true riches and wealth, the success that I desire you to achieve, you need to start thinking differently about aspects such as money, education, risks, and work; you require an "abundance mentality." This type of thinking will allow you to see things differently.

MONEY

Money is a construct that was created as medium of exchange or a store of value; it is what we agree it is. Money was once on the gold standard and actually worth something, but was taken off that standard in 1971, when President Richard Nixon closed the gold window for good. This essentially put us on the dollar standard, which is a *fiat* currency. What that means is that the currency (dollar) is worth whatever the issuing entity (government, monarchy, etc.) says it is worth. This is why you have to start thinking differently about money. If the entity decides that all paper money and like forms are now worthless, then you have nothing of value in terms of physical money.

Many people who are considered poor and middle class mainly see money as a way to get things, while the rich and wealthy see money as a tool to invest. If you think deeply on what I just stated about money being a construct and that it is what we agree it is, then you can essentially get something for nothing because money is kind of an imaginary concept. For the record, when I mentioned that the rich and wealthy see money as a tool to invest, I was not advocating that you should only invest and not enjoy the fruits of your labor. What I meant was that most people choose to buy things out of lack, while the knowledgeable buy out of abundance. This is why an abundance mentality is required, as well as an overall change in your thinking.

If you look at the bigger picture, no one is kept poor because opportunity has been taken away or because certain people have monopolized all the wealth. New money is created daily, and trillions of dollars change hands in a matter of nanoseconds in the financial markets, so stop focusing on what everyone else has and start focusing on what you can get. There is enough to go around for everyone, and it is not difficult if you stop having a limited and competitive mindset.

To become financially successful, you need to stop thinking of spending and think more on investing and acquiring assets. If not then you will continue to stay in the typical lifestyle of working for money, paying taxes, and hoping that circumstances will change (i.e., hitting the lottery or getting a bigger raise). Once you begin to see money for what it is, a tool to invest, you can begin to achieve greater financial success. If you do not know where to start, I suggest beginning with a wonderful book by Jim Rohn titled, *The 7 Strategies of Wealth and Happiness*. This book has excellent advice on how to begin on the road to prosperity and will delve further into details on certain subjects than we have space for in this book.

EDUCATION

As you may have noticed in the text the words rich, wealthy, and financially successful have been used interchangeably. These words are all subjective; therefore, I encourage you to have an operational definition for yourself. For me, wealth is about having an abundance of money extending two or more generations, while being rich is about having enough to cover yourself and one generation; financially successful means having security for your lifetime, but for the purpose of this book the words will essentially be equal so insert the word that fits your goals.

I am a firm believer that it is not possible to live a really complete and successful life unless you have some similitude of financial success. You can be happy with what you have and live a decent life, but you still need money. If that is the case, then why not live life and enjoy it to the fullest?

Making money is not difficult in today's time, especially with the advent of the Internet. Instead of browsing social sites and posting selfies, why not use two of the world's most powerful tools – your brain and the Internet – to make thousands, or even millions, of dollars. Information is at its most accessible unlike when I was coming up and had to go to the library and check out books, read newspapers, or look at reviews and encyclopedias just to get information.

Educating yourself on a subject lead to wisdom and wisdom leads to abundance. I can attest to this because I wanted to learn anything I could on the subject of finance. I was ignorant on the subject until I started reading and getting the knowledge. My education began with two books; one was *The Complete Day Trader* and the other was *The Richest Man in Babylon*. Ever since I began my journey, I have been expanding my education into sources such as trading and investing in securities, such as stocks, dividends, commodities, futures and options, real estate, debt, and other financial systems. My desire to learn and change my socioeconomic status outweighed the situation that I was facing at the beginning, which was prison. I began learning because I did not want to have to be at the mercy of some employer supplying my needs, money, or "job security." If you want to succeed, then your desire needs to be stronger than the need to only save, hang out with family and friends, or live paycheck to paycheck.

Achieving financial success is no different from doing simple math; they both require a process that must be followed to achieve an end result. The only difference is that math is considered a science with steps that leads to the same results, while achieving financial success is a blend of science and art, whereby you can follow steps or create your own to get the same results. To get where I am trying to take you, it does not matter where you come from. Anyone can achieve financial success if they have the ability to think and understand key principles; "like causes" will produce "like effects."

RISKS

During 2018, I read an article in *USA Today* that had a survey stating that 61 percent of high-net-worth men achieved their wealth by taking risks, while 39 percent claimed it was luck. Looking deeper into this, you will see that risk was involved with the 39 percent of men as well because some sort of action had to have been taken that involved some form of risk in hopes that it would pay off. Most people do not take risks because they are afraid, they will fail. The ones who are financially successful may have been afraid as well, but most knew that they had already failed if they chose to do nothing at all.

I am not saying that you should risk everything you have on some investment with the hopes that it will work; that would be insane. What I am saying is that if you have sufficient information on an opportunity and the capital to support making the investment, yet you do nothing then you have failed, you have failed because you did not take the necessary risk to ensure greater financial success. I can give you a perfect example from my own life whereby I missed out on an opportunity because I was too afraid to take a risk.

There was a house in the Atlanta area around the year 2011 that was in foreclosure. The house was to be sold for roughly $300,000. This house was in a good neighborhood but needed some repairs. At the time I was a twenty-one-year-old Sergeant in the Army with a wife and four kids. I could have used my VA loan to purchase the property and with the housing allowance I received for being married I could have easily covered the expenses.

Looking back, I realize that I had the courage to enlist in the military during wartime and deploy to two combat zones but could not muster the courage to invest in my family's future. I made all kinds of excuses as to why I should not purchase the property, even after I had someone reliable give me the inside scoop on it.

Someone else ended up purchasing the property and fixing it up nicely. A few years later it would sell for $1,500,000. I missed out on a major opportunity to make major profits because I was too afraid to take a risk; do not let this be you.

There is a conglomerate of books that can help you understand any subject relating to finance as well as audio books, podcasts, and YouTube videos. The Small Business Administration is another useful tool that can help with its multitude of resources available. In this day and age there is no need to be poor or working class if you truly desire a better life and are willing to take action. The day you stop learning is the day you become ignorant because it is impossible to know everything about one particular subject.

This is where you will have to utilize one of your most valuable assets: time. To quote Jim Rohn, "Time is our most valuable asset, yet we tend to waste it, kill it, and spend it rather than invest it." I believe that if you invest your time wisely into learning the ins and outs of how to become financially successful and take the necessary actions, then you have no choice but to reap what you sow; knowing the process of getting rich or wealthy is not enough to get you there. You have to believe you can acquire the status you seek, change your thinking pattern, develop new habits, and actually apply the knowledge.

WORK

Most people constantly gripe about how the wealthy do not pay taxes or pay fewer taxes than "ordinary" people. The truth is that this is legal through certain tax advantages the government offers. This will be covered in a later chapter, but for now you should know that it is a process for becoming and staying financially successful. There are opportunities and investments galore that allow you to take advantage of the same tax breaks and loopholes as the wealthy. However, instead of making a fortune by doing a little research and work, most people want to take what others have worked hard or smart for and complain about what the next person has that he or she does not. In today's society people would rather scam, sue, cheat, or steal from another person for financial gain than utilize the resources (your brain, Internet, or books) available to follow in the footsteps of the successful.

It is important to note that financially successful people have their money work for them and not the other way around; no one gets rich working for wages. This is because of the vicious cycle of you working to pay someone else first (the government) and not yourself. You are, in essence, dependent on someone else providing for you (your employer) instead of providing for yourself. Hence the old adage "It's not how much you make, but how much you get to keep." The ending part to this saying is what will make you financially successful.

The rich and wealthy know how to make money work for them by using other people's money, commonly known as OPM. They also reinvest any earnings they make back into their assets, which helps aid the power of compounding interest. The poor, working, and middle class all work for money both literally and figuratively. Most, if not all, people in these groups think that money will solve all their problems, so they work harder, longer, and even take multiple jobs just to have "extra" money. Most of the people in these socioeconomic groups do not realize that the more money you make the more Uncle Sam takes, so you still receive less money. That is why investing in an education, a financial one for the purpose of this book, is important.

The poor, working, and middle-class work to buy things with no real value, that is cars, expensive clothes, jewelry, and so on, just to keep up with the so called "Joneses." They want to look the part of having money (refer back to background for my own story). I know because I was one of those people "flexing for the Gram." This "I have to look rich" mentality keeps a lot of people in the same place they are in and probably the same place previous generations were in. Money is their master because it is what tells them when to get up and when to go to work; it keeps them in a cycle of work, earn, and buy, whereby their mindset is to play it safe and never taking risks or the steps necessary to change, and of always being an employee.

If you want to change your outlook from the one described throughout the last few pages, then you have chosen the correct book. I have been through the struggle and trying times. It took me hitting rock bottom to change my way of thinking and invest wisely in myself. That is how the CITRAS™ method was born. This method is a combination of research that I assembled that was common between people who had achieved financial success. This acronym stands for Credit, Investing, Trading, Real estate, Asset protection, and surrounding yourself with likeminded people. I found that these are some of the elements that helped many people in becoming financially successful, which is the aim of this book for any reader.

There are multiple ways to obtain financial success. I developed this method after studying the world of finance, people, and money for the last six years. My knowledge base does not encompass the subjects as a whole, as I am still in infancy in terms of learning. I am not a financial expert. One of my goals with this book is to spread the knowledge that I have attained to the common man or woman without all the technical jargon or up speak. I want you to be able to enjoy having money because it gives you control over your life, and it gives you more confidence. This book is a guide to realizing your freedom, but unless you change your thinking it will not matter how much money you make; you will never be wealthy.

The hardest thing about building wealth is staying true to who you are and not going with the crowd. "The crowd" is made up of ordinary people who panic and are broke – you have to be extraordinary if you want to make it. If you are ready to be extraordinary, then allow me to introduce you to the first subject in the CITRAS™.

1

CREDIT

Credit is the first step of the CITRAS™ method because understanding its usefulness in acquiring financial success allows you to build long-term wealth utilizing your own money, as well as other people's money (OPM). Credit is not the only way to build wealth, but if you desire to use less of your own funds to make more money, then this is one route to take in regard to some of my other methods mentioned in later chapters.

UNDERSTANDING CREDIT

The United States is facing a real problem with debt, and I do not mean the "good" kind that can be utilized to build financial wealth. We, as a nation, are in a deficit. That means we are consuming more goods than we are selling and buying more than we can afford; we are consumers and not owners of goods and services.

I began writing this book in 2019, and at the time the U.S. government was $20 trillion in debt. This is a real problem, not only for the current generation but also for the ones to follow. There is nothing much that we as individuals can do to solve this on a macroeconomic (aggregate) level, but we can solve the problem of debt on a microeconomic (individual) level. Our society has become more reliant on credit, especially with the advent of the credit card and digital currency. Borrowers are aware of the negative impact that defaulting will have on their credit score, which will impact their lives for many years, yet there is still so much negative debt.

To put it another way, credit in the corporate world is not different from having "street cred." Both rely on you being certified or vouched for in your ability to pay, be a person of your word, and having a solid reputation; it essentially boils down to you being trustworthy. Credit is a tool that allows us to enjoy something today with money that we earn in the future, similar to a payday loan or advance. This is an often-misused instrument. It should be used to help ourselves, our family, and once we get wealthy enough our community. Credit should be used to purchase assets or make investments, not liabilities.

GOOD CREDIT AND BAD CREDIT

Using credit is too easy these days. It seems that everyone who has something to sell is offering some type of credit whether it is for a car, business item, or home furniture. The home furniture thing is a major selling point for poor and middle-class people and can cause serious financial problems. Using credit improperly can land you in trouble. This is when you acquire bad debt.

Why is credit trouble so damaging? It is because having a bad credit history will hinder you in getting ahead financially. I can attest to having had "bad" credit. This type of negative credit makes it difficult, but not impossible, to get a mortgage, car loan, insurance, and even a good job. Even if you are able to get a loan, you will more than likely end up having a double-digit interest rate in one of the aforementioned situations, compared to someone with a better score. Bad credit is damaging to wealth creation, causes you to pay more than necessary, and can be avoided with proper education.

As the sub-header states, there are two types of debt: good and bad. Most people are familiar with only one type and that is bad debt. This type of debt is well known because it is highly talked about in regard to credit cards, student loans, and any type of default or delinquencies, such as repossessions or foreclosures. Debt of any kind is highly criticized by some, and you are encouraged to get out of debt and pay for everything in cash. This may be caused by people not truly understanding money or it could be that they do not know how to properly employ the uses of credit or debt.

Whatever the reason, rarely if ever at all do you hear about good debt and its uses. This type of debt may be included in the aggregate debt total that is publicized, but you may never know it because of the doom and gloom information put out about debt. These people tend to think consumers are ignorant, so the whole story is not given – just the part the media would like us to hear. Simply put, good debt is mainly used to acquire assets and things of real value that appreciate (art, rental properties, and stocks) while bad debt is used to purchase liabilities that decrease in value (televisions, personal vehicles, latest cell phone, or expensive clothing).

It is almost impossible in today's society to not incur some form of debt. This means that you will more than likely purchase something on credit, whether it is as small as fuel for your car or something as large as a home. With the advent of the debit and credit cards, along with the ability to make a purchase with your cell phone or wearable device, it is hard not to use credit. The utilization of credit can be a wonderful tool, if used properly.

YOUR CREDIT AND CREDIT REPORT

The traditional key to using other people's money has been your personal credit regarding utilizing financial institutions; thus, making your credit history, or the length of you using credit, the most significant factor. For those of you who are new to the world of credit, these things are very influential in deciding if you can use OPM to build wealth.

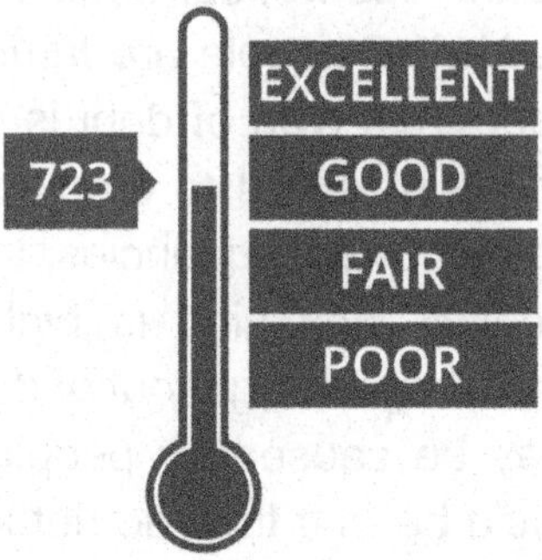

You want to pull a credit report to see if there are any discrepancies on your record, especially if you intend on using OPM. There is a difference between your credit report and your credit history. One is the whole (credit report), while the other is a sum of the whole (credit history). A credit report is typically defined as a combination of your entire financial history and is usually kept track of by the three major bureaus: TransUnion, Experian, and Equifax. These three are the most common companies used by lenders; however, there are other lesser-known credit bureaus out there that track your history.

Most of the bureaus collect the same information, but the companies or institutions, which you are borrowing from may not report to all three bureaus. This will lead to varying scores between the three major agencies. Your score will usually range from a low of 350 to a high of 850; however, with the introduction of the Advantix score and new changes to credit scoring, you can now score well into the 900s. This new scoring system is gaining headway and may soon replace the antiquated FICO score.

There is an overwhelming amount of information that you will need to review and verify if you decide to check your credit report. Fraud is rampant in today's society, so you need to ensure that you have not been a victim of identity theft. The Internet provides you with multiple ways to monitor and check your score, and some of these options are free. Several options that you can utilize include:

- AnnualCreditReport.com: Using this site will allow you to get all three of your reports, but not any of the scores. Getting your score is a paid option for a nominal fee. With that in mind, you are allowed one free report form all bureaus once a year. No, you cannot request one for free in December and a new one in January. "Once a year" means one year from your initial request. So, if you request it in December, you will have to wait until December or later of the following year to request another free report.

  I have been using this option for the last five years and all have been exceptional except TransUnion. During my use, I have always received Experian and Equifax reports without fail, yet TransUnion makes me jump through hoops without getting anything. Last year, 2019, was the first year I received my TransUnion credit report since I began using the site and its form. If you will be using this option, please ensure that you type the exact address into the bar or you may be forced to some off brand site that tries to charge you. You can also Google the site or go to ftc.gov and proceed to the site from there.

- Lifelock: This option is fairly decent. I used this one back in 2012 and was pleased. At the time I was under a paid membership and the scoring was fairly accurate to what creditors pulled. The only thing that I did not like was that you only receive two scores and reports. Also, I only received monthly updates from the start of my membership, so my score lagged if my score increased. There is also a free option for this site for those of you who do not want to pay.

- My Fico: This option provides you with all three reports and scores, but it is one of the more expensive options. In this case expensive is not always the better choice, so choose carefully. There are other options that will provide you the same service for less.

- Credit Karma: This option is good for checking you credit with the drawback that you only receive two reports and scores. Plus, there is a ton of advertising with the free option, much like Pandora and their free music service. I tried this option last year and liked what was provided. You will need to ensure that you can either recall past debts or have an old report on hand. You will have to answer questions about your history in order to access the information. If you cannot recall the correct answers, you will be kicked out of the site and forced to start over. Other than that, the site is good enough for its intended use.

Improving or having good credit is a step in CITRAS™, because it assists in your ability to attain financial freedom or wealth easier. This tool will allow you to effectively utilize the other tools, such as investing, trading, and real estate at a maximum capacity; therefore, it is important to understand your credit report.

The most influential credit scores that lenders use is your FICO score. This scoring system was created by a company called Fair Isaac Corporation, hence the name FICO, to judge a person's creditworthiness. When it comes to the subject of credit scoring, there has been varying opinions on the average credit score, but it is mostly centered between the mid-600s and the low-700s. The factors that contribute to calculating your FICO score include payment history, debt account, history length, types of credit, and new credit.

- Payment history: This portion of your credit will include things such as late payments, derogatory debt, missed payments, as well as any past obligations that you have met; it is a mixture of both good and bad debt, mostly good if you have made payments on time and vice versa. This portion of your credit calculations accounts for 35 percent of your overall score! This is why it is important to pay your bills early or on time.

Payment history tells the creditors that you can met or have met your financial obligations for its duration. Missing even one payment can have a profound effect on your score. It can potentially mean a drop from a mid-700 score to a score in the high-600s. Ultimately this area shows that you are responsible person, and it is one of those implied critiques that you are judged on. Note: Missed payments can be modified if you had difficulties at one point in your life but still continued to pay the obligation. It will take some effort, but you should start with sending a goodwill letter detailing how you were in a bad situation and that you still met your obligation, and then ask to have the derogatory mark removed.

- Debt accounts: This is the next largest section of your report that is heavily weighed. It accounts for 30 percent of your score and includes any accounts that you owe. As you can already see, paying your bills on time and keeping them up to date carries a lot of weight towards your score. Payment history and debt accounts go hand-in-hand.

- History length: One would think that the longer a person has had credit the better the credit score, but that is not always the case. A longer credit history can prove that you are more likely to pay your debts than someone with a weaker history; on the other hand, a person with a short history can have a better score if she has paid on time and has not maxed out any lines of credit, such as home equity lines or credit cards. This area of your credit report accounts for only 15 percent, which is still significant but not as heavily weighed as payment history or debt accounts. History length shows that you are established and is one of the reasons it is advised not to close old or unused credit lines. Closing them can damage your score, especially if the accounts are in good standings.

- Types of credit: This portion accounts for 10 percent of your score and refers to the different types of credit lines you have available. This can include charge cards, car loans, credit cards, or a mortgage. Basically, lenders want to see that you have more than one type of credit available for use and that you are not abusing a single line of usage, such as credit cards.

- New credit: This section also accounts for 10 percent of your score and refers to any recently opened accounts or hard inquiries. Recently opened accounts and multiple hard inquiries for new credit can be seen as a potential sign to lenders that you are high risk.

  Recall that payment history, debt accounts, and history length account for a total of 80 percent of your credit, so any new line of credit will not be established long enough to count or have a payment history. New accounts will not show up on your credit for at least 90 days after you have opened and established the account. On the other hand, hard inquiry requests from companies that have pulled your credit to evaluate you for a line of credit will stay on your report for two years, so space out the timing for new credit applications.

Credit scoring plays a major role in just about everything. You have a credit score evaluation for getting a car loan, mortgage loan, insurance, a job, and even utilities. Our life essentially revolves around numbers – from your social security number to your income to your height, weight, and credit. Now that we have discussed credit and how it is important to building financial success, I will give you tips and information on how to build or improve your score.

IMPROVING YOUR CREDIT

As you know, your credit score will be used in almost every facet of your life to evaluate your creditworthiness. This can range from applying for a loan, credit card, or getting utilities for your home or apartment. When these companies evaluate you, there will be varying opinions on what is considered a "good" score. Generally, a score between 700 and 749 is good, with anything above 750 or higher being considered excellent. If you have "bad" credit or no credit at all, there are some steps you can take to get on the road to better credit and financial success.

You should start building a credit history as soon as possible, if you do not have one. It will not matter that you have excellent income and money in the bank if you have a low credit score. The records of your checking and savings accounts will not help you on the road to financial success as they do not show creditors enough evidence of how you may handle credit.

If you have no credit or a low credit score, one way you can begin to build credit is to be added as an authorized user on someone else's credit card, like a relative or close friend. The original owner will ultimately be responsible for any charges, so ensure that you both are on the same page when it comes to how the card can be used and how it will be paid. This option is great if the person who owns the card has a habit of paying on time. You benefit from the person's creditworthiness while boosting your own score.

I have an associate who used this option, and his credit score has greatly improved due to the original owner being so good with credit. My associate now has great credit as well as untapped lines of credit on his card, so he can start his business once he leaves the military.

Another option you can use is getting a secured card. I can personally attest to this option. I had a Wells Fargo Secured Card back in 2013 after returning from deployment so that I could start rebuilding my credit. My credit was in the mid-500s before I got the card. By using it properly, my score was close to 700 before I was incarcerated. This was because I had started paying bills early or on time, as well as utilizing my credit card properly.

With a secured card, you provide an upfront deposit (collateral) and the company extends you a line of credit equal to the deposit. For me, I deposited $300 on my secured card. There was no limit to what I could have deposited, but I felt that was a good enough limit to start with. By getting and utilizing my secured card, I was able to demonstrate I could handle credit responsibly, which in turn helped me establish a better credit history. If the issuer sees that you are responsible, you may qualify for an unsecured card later on. And with most cards, the deposit is refundable after a certain period of time (assuming you did not overdraft the limit and not pay).

With Wells Fargo, I qualified for an unsecured card with a $1,500 limit after one year. There are options besides Wells Fargo, and I am not endorsing them, but I banked with them while I was in the military, so I deemed it a good choice. You can check with your local bank, credit union, or search online to find other options for a secured card. Before choosing just any old, secured card, ensure that the issuer will report to all three credit bureaus; you would not want all your hard work to go unnoticed while rebuilding your credit.

Besides getting a secured card from your financial institution, you can also apply for small loans to help build up your credit. The loans are usually small amounts that you can pay back within a few months to a year. Most financial institutions may have a program in place such as this, so ask your teller or any bank associate about it the next time you visit. My ex-wife used this option to help rebuild her credit. Before I was incarcerated and we divorced, her credit was just as bad as mine, if not worse. Roughly two years ago she told me she had begun to rebuild her credit and getting small loans was one way she had done it. Last time we spoke she told me her score was in the high-600s. There are many ways to get on your feet, or back on your feet, if you so desire.

The options I have mentioned are great; however, there are other steps you must take to ensure that they will work. For one, you should look to pay your bills on time. The best way to maintain a good credit rating, especially after being approved for any type of loan or credit card, is to never miss a payment. This is simple information, but it is also one of the simplest to screw up.

Of course, never missing a payment will not always be the case. Situations will happen, but this too can be resolved. Remember, you can still pay your bills and later request the delinquency be removed or simply call and explain your situation. Before you get to that point though, you should be keeping an eye on your spending. Recall that debt accounts will account for 30 percent of your credit score; your goal is to build up your credit, not to dig yourself deeper into debt.

Also, do not open too many lines of credit at once. This will cause those hard inquiries to show up on your report, which can drop your score. And they stay on your history for two years. The final step in ensuring this all works out and that you are on the path to financial success is to check your report on a regular basis. You can do this annually through annualcreditreport.com or whatever sources you like that provides you a report and score, such as Credit Karma.

Once you are on the right track and have improved your credit score, it will become easier to achieve financial success through other methods mentioned in this book. The next option you can use to build your wealth is through investing, which is the subject of the next chapter.

2

INVESTING

What is the first thing you think of when you hear the term “invest”? Most people think of stocks, mutual funds, and bonds. If these are some of the investment securities that come to mind when you hear the term invest, then you are not alone. These types of investments are known as “traditional investments,” along with other securities such as exchange-traded funds (ETFs) and annuities. These traditional investments are highly touted by the investment industry as ways to plan for retirement or any other future goal; however, if you dig deeper into the subject of investing and the different classes, you will find another class that is just as lucrative called “alternative investments.”

Alternative investments are rarely mentioned because the industry brokers cannot make big commissions off of them as they can with traditional investments. This class includes investments other than stocks, bonds, and mutual funds. Alternative investments can include, but are not limited to, tax liens or deeds, peer-to-peer lending, foreign exchange (FX), futures and options, or commodities. The list is pretty long and can be highly profitable, however, you should only trade or invest in securities that you are comfortable with and have some sort of experience or training in.

Most, if not all, of these investments are high risk/high rewards and can wipe out your account in a matter of seconds. When investing in any sort of financial security, you should only invest with capital that you can afford to lose and not with funds allocated for items such as mortgage, insurance, or food. Also, you should not be investing or possibly trading (which will be discussed in Chapter 3) with funds borrowed from a financial institution, due to the possibility of a major loss. This will put you further in a bind and cause undue financial stress. Some of these securities can be purchased at a discount, even ones that pose a high risk.

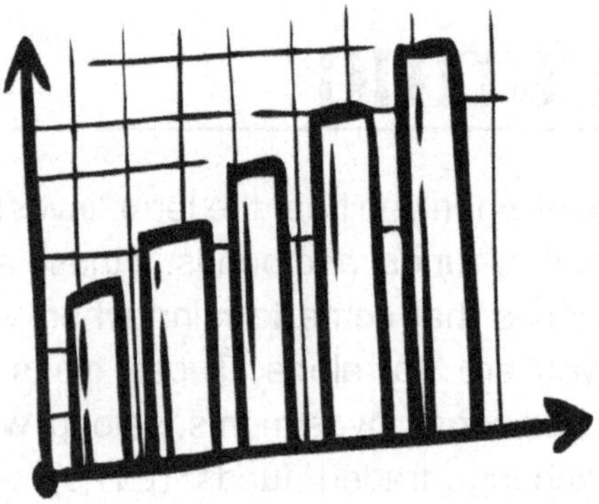

As with anything you purchase or invest in, there can be no risk without reward. There is an opportunity to make money in both traditional and alternative investments, but this may not be for everyone. Choosing what is right for you will depend on several factors such as capital available, appetite for risk, motivation, and time. If you have these things readily available, then it is time to learn about both types of investments.

TRADITIONAL INVESTMENTS

Stocks

Purchasing stocks allows you to own a piece of the company, so when it makes a profit you also make a profit. It is essentially like being a business owner without the hassle of running the day-to-day operations. This allows for what is known as passive income, or mailbox money, which is income that comes from investments such as stocks, real estate, or owning a business where you can make money regardless of if you are there or not. Stocks can be bought and held for the long term, but with the changing society and tax laws, you must decide how best to manage your portfolio.

There are myriad ways to invest in stocks along with multiple types of stocks. This can range from categories such as growth, value, defensive, or international stocks, just to name a few. When you choose to invest in the stock market it is more than just picking a good company you like; it involves having knowledge of the market or company as well as having a solid plan for investing. For instance, it would not be proper to invest in a growth company that offers no dividend if you are looking to supplement your income. It is imperative that you get the knowledge on the types of investments you are interested in. There are tons of books, podcasts, and research dedicated to educating you on this subject.

When or if you decide to invest, you should follow and adhere to certain investing mantras:

- You should *never* invest all of your capital into one stock or have only stocks in your portfolio. This will cause you to take a major loss in the event the market as a whole decides to go bearish or go down.

- You should maintain some sort of savings or cash holding because stocks are not a replacement for having emergency cash on hand, especially if the market tanks. Having cash on hand can also mean that you are able to purchase quality stock at a discount while everyone else is panicking and selling.

- Ensure that you do your own research on any investment while maintaining a healthy dose of skepticism about advice being given.

- Buy low and sell high. Any profit is always better than no profit when it comes to the world of investing and trading. When investing, any type of security whether stocks or bonds, should ultimately be seen as a business and once the price is right or high enough, then it should be sold. You should not become emotionally attached to any investment. You are in the market to make money.

- Follow what the market is giving you and use it to your advantage, because other investors surely are.

TYPES OF STOCKS

There are several types of stocks, but for the purpose of this book I will introduce you to only three, which are growth stocks, small capitalization, and income stocks.

Growth Stocks: Growth stocks are considered riskier than value or income stocks, yet they tend to grow faster than the stocks of other companies. To be considered a growth stock, a company must consistently show growth over time. An example of a growth stock would be Amazon. This company has consistently grown over a long period of time and has proven itself to be one hell of a market leader. One of the most important parts of a growth stock is that they tend to not offer a dividend, so that any profits made may be reinvested into growing the company and thus increasing the price per share.

When looking to invest in a growth stock, you should look for several things within the company such as research and development (R&D), market leadership, brand strength, any fundamental information, and who is buying shares of this company; these will give you a better understanding of what you are looking to purchase. For instance, a company like Apple tends to spend money on R&D so that it can develop new products. They also have many loyal customers who are willing to wait in line to pay thousands for new phones and devices. They are considered a market leader, continue to show growth, and have a super-strong brand.

By looking at a company's fundamentals, you can evaluate the strength of the company and its finances. This information can easily be obtained through sites such as Yahoo! Finance, Morningstar, *The Wall Street Journal*, or any other financial source. Utilizing any of the aforementioned tools will allow you to compare company against company to see where each rank amongst its industry or sector (*e.g.,* Apple versus Samsung).

Looking at a company's fundamentals involves looking at its balance sheet, statement of cash flows, income statement or other data to see how strong the company is. Remember, if the company is making a profit so are you. As far as who is buying the stock, you can check the daily average volume and compare it to the current volume. This information can be found in publications such as *Consumer Reports* or any of the previously mentioned sites. This is equally important because more buyers or demand for your stock makes the price rise.

Small Capitalization Stocks: Also known as "small caps," these stocks have a capitalization of less than $1 billion. Capitalization refers to the number of share the company has issued multiplied by the price per share of the stock. For instance, if Company A has 10 million shares outstanding and the price per share is $10, then its capitalization is $100 million (10 million x $10). Small caps tend to show the greatest growth of all stocks, like the small businesses created daily that help contribute to jobs and economic growth. Just because these companies are small does not mean that they will not experience explosive growth.

Even if this is the case, you should still evaluate a company's financial strength to ensure that it is a positive investment. If you can pick winners from this type of stock, then it could be the next Apple or Google; however, do not bank on this alone. Another area of small caps can be "penny" stocks, depending on your definition.

The Securities Exchange Commission (SEC) defines a penny stock as "having value of less the five dollars." These types of securities will allow you to get more bang for your buck, especially if they are winners. Small caps can be risky if you do not understand them; this type of investing is mainly for sophisticated investors. Penny stocks are considered more of a micro-cap investment, but the definition is subjective and should pertain to your situation.

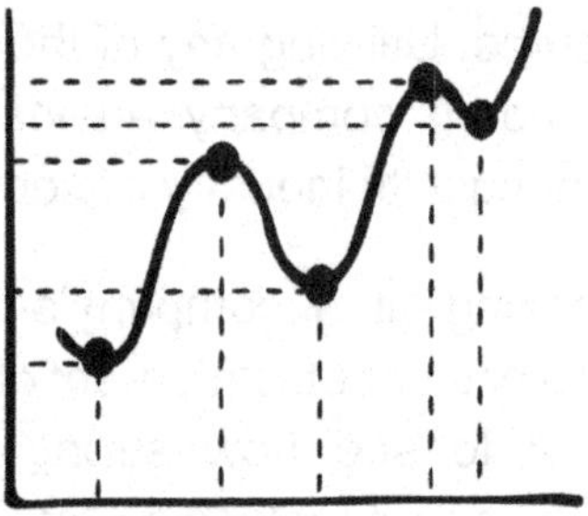

Invest at your own risk, but if you decide to invest then you should know that small caps going public through an initial public offering (IPO) is not certain; this is another reason why they are risky. Most people choose small cap stocks with the belief that is will make it big if it hits the market.

When evaluating a company that is considered a penny stock, you want to ensure that the company is making money. If you recall the company Theranos, it was supposed to be a unicorn and was hyped to be the next big revolutionizing thing, but it eventually failed because, among other things, it was not making money.

In regard to that, a company should have been in business and making a profit for at least three years minimum before you decide to invest hard-earned cash. Do not go investing into a company just because you think it will make a profit or because it sounds like a good company; get hard facts on the security and then decide if you should invest (remember investing mantras 3 and 4).

Income Stocks: These are the type of investments known to most as dividend stocks or as dividend investing. They provide you with a regular flow of cash (dividends) and can be appropriate for different investors. This type of investing is most common amongst new investors, retirees, or dividend reinvestment plan (DRIP) investors.

A DRIP investor is someone who accumulates partial or whole shares with an initial investment as low as $10. This can add up substantially if you make daily, weekly, or monthly investments through what is known as "dollar cost averaging." With this type of investing, you can purchase stocks whether the market is going up or down. This in turn lowers your average purchasing costs and allows you to purchase more shares.

For example, if you were to invest $100 one week into Company A and it costs $10 a share, you would get 10 shares if there are no costs associated with purchasing them. Let us say that you do this on a weekly basis, so next week when you invested $100 the price was now $10.50. Now you are only able to purchase 9.524 shares, which brings you to a total of 19.534 shares. In your third week the stock drops to $8.50 a share, so this week your $100 investment allows you to purchase 11.765 shares for a total of 31.298 shares. If you were to stop at this point your total average cost per share is $10 even, though you purchased at three different prices. You get the average by adding the costs (10 + 11.50 + 8.50 = 30) and dividing by the number of times you purchased (30 ÷ 3 = 10).

Income investing is better for long-term investing goals and is usually purchased for nothing more than income, unlike growth stocks that are purchased for their spectacular growth. As I previously mentioned, these income stocks usually produce a dividend that is money the company has decided to issue to the owner(s) of the stock, from company profits. These dividends are mainly paid quarterly or every three months, but there are some companies that issue dividends only annually.

To understand how this works imagine that a company pays a dividend of $2 per share. If the company issues the dividend on a quarterly basis, then you will receive $0.50 per share every three months. As with the previous example, you would receive $15.65 per quarter for your 31.298 shares, which can be used to purchase more shares or be returned to you as income. This is what you can expect if the company does not change its policy; however, dividends are not guaranteed and can be discontinued at any time to either spur growth or keep the doors open. I once had a company lower its dividend to $0.01 per share so it could restructure and lower its debt load. Nevertheless, income stocks are good investments to have because they have historically equaled or exceeded the rate of inflation, which benefits you as an investor.

When evaluating a dividend company, you want to look at its financial strength in the same manner you would when deciding whether to invest for growth, because financial strength is important if you are looking for this income to support you.

There are, at a minimum, three things you should look at when evaluating an income stock: dividend yield, payout ratio, and bond ratings for that particular company. The dividend yield is the rate of return that the stock gives you in the form of a dividend or a percentage of return based on the price of the stock. This allows you to compare different investments to see which one will give you a better return for your money. You can find the yield by using the following formula: (dividend income) ÷ (stock investment) = (dividend yield).

You can do this yourself or easily find it on any of the previously mentioned sites. It is important to note that the price of a stock changes constantly, so your yield will change as well; the dividend may not change at all, but because of the change in price your yield will change. For example, imagine that you purchased shares of Company C, which traded for $15 per share a year ago, with a dividend of $0.60. This would make your yield at that particular time 4 percent when utilizing the above formula. Now let us say that it is a year later, and that same stock has risen in price to $25 per share with the same dividend of $0.60, what is the current yield? Using the formula, you find out that it is now only 2.4 percent and not the same 4 percent it was a year ago. The price now does not offer an attractive dividend compared to a year ago, so it may be best to look at other opportunities.

Another useful piece of information for evaluating income stock is the payout ratio. This ratio tells you what percentage of the company earnings are being paid out in the form of dividends. This allows you to see if the company is paying out too much in dividends, which could spell trouble.

Generally speaking, a company that is paying out roughly 60 percent or less of company earnings is a safe percentage. Remember, dividends are not always permanent, so in order to gauge whether your company will continue to payout dividends, you need to check its cash flows from operations and compare it to the earnings; a company that is paying out less than the aforementioned 60 percent will still have room to grow if earnings fall more than 10 percent. Nothing is guaranteed, so keep a lookout on any income investments you may have.

If you are truly interested in income investing, then you should keep an eye on the company's bond rating. Bond ratings help offer you useful insight on the financial strength of the company. Agencies such as Moody's or Standard & Poor's (S&P) can provide you with bond ratings. This rating lets you know if the company is able to repay its debt or if the company is so financially weak that it will default on its obligations and fall into "junk" bond status. The highest ratings for bonds are AAA or Triple A and Baa3 and flows to a low of D, which are considered junk bonds. Bonds are extensive and sometimes good investments, which is why they are the next type of security to be discussed.

Bonds

Bonds are considered good and sometimes great investments for people who like safety. With a bond, you essentially get an IOU from the company, or whatever agency issues the bond, in return for lending it your money. Any person retaining this bond will receive a certain amount of interest that the entity promises to pay.

The list is too exhaustive to go into detail, since I do not consider this a comprehensive guide; however, there are sources dedicated to bond interest in explicit detail. For now, a bond is a debt that in the event of a company or entity defaulting or going bankrupt, you have priority in terms of getting repaid over people who may own stocks. In essence, a bond is similar to income stocks in that you receive a steady stream of income with the only exception being that you receive your initial capital back once the bond expires, is called, or reaches maturity. There are some key informational nuggets that you should know about bonds before investing in them:

- Bonds can be issued in either investment grade or junk grade; I mentioned Triple A and junk bonds earlier in the book. Investment grade bonds carry little-to-no risk and are usually top-rated Triple A to B bonds. Junk bonds or high-yield bonds are the ones that carry high risks and will include your low to lowest rated bonds. Junk bonds have the highest risk of default but give you the highest rate of return for that risk; top-rated bonds can default as well.

- Bonds can be issued at a premium (higher face value) or at a discount (lower face value). Many factors will determine the price of a bond if you decide to purchase on the secondary market. Interest rates and inflation are a few factors that influence the cost of bonds. This is an extensive subject. For now, it is important just to remember these key nuggets.

- A bond will always, I repeat *always*, be issued at a certain face value or amount. The face value, which has other known names such as par value or principal, will more often than not be at a value of $1,000.

- There can be instances where you, as an investor, will be able to purchase a bond directly from the issuing entity (i.e., government, company, or state) and be able to sell it back to them. This is known as the primary market, but most likely you will end up purchasing from the secondary market through either a broker or a bank.

- Every bond you purchase will pay a fixed value (rate of interest) over the life of the bond, which is why bonds are commonly known as "fixed income securities."

Where Do Bonds Come From?

There are millions upon millions of bonds issued by different government agencies, corporations, foreign governments, and so on. I see bonds being issued regularly when reading *The Wall Street Journal*. For example, the United States Treasury issues bonds to raise money for different things such as infrastructure or defense. This is how certain things can get built instead of the government raising taxes, yet taxes progressively rise on the income we make. I am not going to go down that rabbit hole; that is a subject for some other author. For now, just know that there is a plethora of treasury bonds to invest in, so do your homework on the one(s) that fit your portfolio.

Other issuers of bonds can include cities, counties, and states. These bonds are known as municipal bonds or "munis." Municipal bonds are used to raise funds for specific day-to-day needs, and they may provide you with tax benefits. I advise you to consult with an accountant or tax consultant on specific bonds and their benefits before choosing to purchase.

There are also what were considered quasi-government agencies such as the Federal National Mortgage Association (FNMA or Fannie Mae) that issue bonds. I say they are considered quasi-government owned because during the Great Recession of 2008 this organization became government owned through the Troubled Asset Relief Program (TARP) and is now owned by the Treasury. Back to the subject at hand, there are also corporations that issue bonds such as General Electric. In regard to bonds, corporate bonds are much riskier and tend to compensate investor by offering a higher interest rate.

Most bonds are issued with maturities of life spans up to a period of 30 years; however, there are entities that now issue them in longer spans. Bonds that have a maturity of less than five years are known as short bonds. If the maturity is between 5-12 years, then they are known as intermediate bonds, while anything longer than 12 years is called a long bond. Generally speaking, the longer the maturity the higher the interest paid. This is due to the fact that your capital is tied up for longer periods of time, and if the economy changes and better opportunities are present, then you are somewhat compensated through the higher interest rate.

Each type of bond will have its pros and cons that should be evaluated based on your investment goals. Each will also have a different yield, and if you are investing for income, then this will be how you determine it.

Yield

There are different types of yields that you should be aware of: knowing the yield will tell you the amount of income to expect. This can be complicated at times, so do not get stuck looking for yield only.

One form of yield that you should become familiar with is called coupon yield. This type of yield is fairly easy to understand and is commonly referred to as the "coupon rate." For example, if a $1,000 bond has a coupon yield of 6 percent, then it will pay you $60 a year.

Current yield is another type of yield you should be familiar with; it is the inverse of coupon yield. You can find current yield by taking the coupon rate and dividing it by the price of the bond. To keep things simple, I will use the previous example, so if a bond with a face value of $1,000 had a rate of 6 percent, you would get $60. Now imagine that the same bond now sold at a discount value of $980 with the same rate, your current yield would now equal 6.12 percent. You get this by dividing the coupon yield of $60 by the value of $980, which ends up being 0.061224. Once converted to a percentage the answer is 6.12 percent. You can also do this if the bond sold at a premium of $1020. Knowing the formula and how it works, you can easily find out that the current yield equals 5.88 percent. This yield is helpful if you want to get a picture of your monthly return over the life of the bond.

As I stated before, yield can be complicated so when investigating an investment, it is wise to consult with a professional. If you want to dig deeper into other forms of yields you should check out the 30-day yield, yield-to-call, and yield-to-maturity.

Each type of bond and its issuing agency allows for different tax exemptions and implications. You should check with your local accounting professional to see which type of bond is suitable for your portfolio. You can also do your own research through select web sites beforehand so that you can know what questions to ask. Sites such as sec.gov or ratings sites such as Moody's or S&P can help you gauge the market for bonds.

So far, I have only gone over so-called "safe," traditional investing. This can include stocks, bonds, mutual funds, and ETFs. I enjoy utilizing these securities, especially when planning for the long term; however, in order to achieve better results it may be necessary to take risks, mainly through diversification. Earlier I mentioned a survey that appeared in *USA Today* that stated how 61 percent of the men interviewed indicated that they achieved their wealth through risk taking. These risks were not just random but calculated risks, which means that the pros of the investment outweighed the cons for these individuals; this is where alternative investments can come into play.

ALTERNATIVE INVESTMENTS

The next few pages will introduce you to a different form of investing, known as "alternative investments." Most of these investments will deal with debt; someone else's bad debt could allow you the opportunity to make a profit if you know what to do with it. Before entering into alternative investments, it is necessary to get educated on the investments outside of the information that I will provide you.

As I have mentioned before, this is not a comprehensive book to all things wealth related; this book was created to serve as an informational and motivational book to help you pursue financial success by taking advantage of the resources. When I mention alternative investing throughout this book, I do not mean this as a way to take advantage of people, but as a way to profit from debt in the same manner that other investors or businesses will.

If you read the chapter on credit, then you know that there are two forms of debt: good and bad. Alternative investing deals with both forms and can be a great tool for wealth building. The two forms of alternative investments that I will briefly discuss are peer-to-peer lending and tax liens or deeds. There are myriad other forms of alternative investments, but for simplicity only these two will be discussed.

Peer-to-Peer Lending (P2P)
This is just what the name implies, you loan money to other people in need. You are essentially like a bank or other lending institution that loans out money and collect interest. It is said that net returns of 5-10 percent can be made from your computer by utilizing this form of alternative investing. This is superior to the normal returns you may be getting from a savings account, certificate of deposit, or another instrument.

There are pros and cons to this type of investing, as with any type. Loaning money through online sites makes your funds unsecured, so there is no collateral to cover any losses you may incur. It is no different than if you borrowed money that is not collateralized by an asset and decided not to pay it back or maybe "loaning" it to a family member who never returns the money, plus you do not receive any interest. If this style still interests, you then you should check with your state to see if this is available to you.

In some states you have to be a "qualified investor," which means you must make between $200,000 a year ($300,000 for couples) or have a net worth of $1,000,000. A qualified investor is believed to know the risks inherent to any investment he or she is partaking in and can recover more quickly than someone who is not a qualified investor.

There are several sites dedicated to P2P lending, so you should take the necessary time to investigate and research the one that fits your investment goals. Sites such as Prosper, Lending Club, and others offer a range of loans that you can invest in. With these sites there are low risk loans that are considered "safe" as well as high risk loans that compensate you by offering a higher rate of return.

The section on bonds mentioned Triple A and junk bonds; it is essentially no different with investing in peer lending. Your "triple A" loans will be the safe, low-risk loans while your "junk" loans are the ones that are high risk, high reward.

Investing in these loans is very simple and sometimes you can get started with as little as $25. As with investing in traditional securities, you should only use capital that you can afford to lose; do not let greed be your downfall on your way to financial success. Peer lending is an excellent investment because billions of dollars are loaned out every year for things such as emergencies, business, weddings, or simple "surprise" expenses like a flat tire or blown engine, so why not earn better interest on your money while increasing your personal financial wealth?

One of the best parts of peer lending is that you can choose what you would like to contribute. You can also reinvest your capital and interest back into more loans and setting up an account is fairly easy. We know that society is severely dependent on credit – just look at the deficit. There are multiple sources out there dedicated to educating you on the subject of P2P lending, and just like any investment I have mentioned, it is best to consult a professional about your tax liabilities and implications before making any rash decisions.

Tax Liens and Deeds

This wonderful little gem got me real excited when I first began to learn about it. There are several advantages that this investment has over other forms – anyone can do it, it has priority over *all* other debt, and there is a very small chance that you could end up owning some real estate! On top of that, you can earn up to double-digit interest rates on your capital investment. Yes, you read that correctly: double digit interest rates! Check with your individual state or whatever state you choose to invest in as to how tax liens are sold. In some states this instrument is called a tax deed. For example, Missouri is a tax-lien state, while my home state of Georgia is a tax-deed state.

Tax liens are sold by the tax collectors to help make up for any unpaid taxes on the property; this is because the local county where the property is located depends on those taxes to provide amenities and services like schools or roads. For anyone new to this information, a tax lien is an instrument that is used to secure the repayment of debt by imposing a legal claim on the collateral. Basically, the government or some official entity forecloses on the property and auctions it off so that it can get paid.

Tax liens and deeds are a great way to try and gain property at a severely steep discount, especially since real estate is part of the CITRAS™ method and will be discussed more in chapter four. Utilizing either a tax lien or deed makes this type of investment more of a business than a hobby, due to long-term commitments such as time, capital, research, and possible management of any property. You should seriously consider if this is the right investment for you before venturing into this arena.

There are differences you should be aware of between a tax lien and a tax deed. As mentioned before, a lien is a legal restriction on the property to secure repayment of debt. With that, the original owner still maintains possession and ownership of the property until he or she redeems (pays off) the lienholder (you or the municipality). There may be a waiting period before you can foreclose on the property, so check with your local county in regard to specifications.

Depending on the wait time, you will have to pay any subsequent taxes on the property until it can be redeemed; this allows you to keep priority on the property. If you do not, then someone else can pay the new or current years taxes and wipe you out of position. It is important to ensure that you are getting the property free and clear of all other liens if you are able to redeem it, otherwise you will become responsible for those liens and any profit that you had hoped to gain could be wiped out. This can be avoided by having a title company do a quick title search.

Tax deeds, on the other hand, allow you as an investor to acquire a deed on the property rather than a lien. Deeds vary from state to state, so check with your county or municipality to see how either a lien or deed works.

When dealing with tax deeds, this type of investment can come in one or two forms: redeemable or nonredeemable. They are like night and day, so ensure you know which type you are purchasing. A redeemable tax deed allows the property owner a certain amount of tine to pay off any taxes that are in arrears or the person will lose the property. It is similar to a tax lien except you become the owner by virtue of the deed, if the original owner fails to pay you, without having to go through a lengthy foreclosure process.

A nonredeemable deed allows you as the investor to take ownership at the end of the sale. As you can probably guess from the name nonredeemable, there is no redemption period. If you are purchasing any type of deed, ensure that you have done your homework because you will be liable for any and everything related to the property. Due diligence is your best friend when it comes to investing. One a final note, consult with a qualified lawyer before investing in tax liens or deeds so that you can avoid any potential pitfalls associated with them.

This concludes the section on investing. I hope this did not overwhelm you because there is more to come. The information contained within is not meant to scare or overload you, it is meant to inspire you and show you that you have other options besides what is being publicized or from merely working and saving. The next chapter will focus on trading, so keep an open mind and prepare to learn.

3

TRADING

This chapter will introduce you to the concept of several financial securities that can be traded, short or long term, to help you reach your financial goals. You can trade just about anything on the market, but for the purpose of this book I will only introduce three instruments for trading: options, commodities, and the foreign exchange market (forex).

For anyone new to trading, it allows for certain advantages and disadvantages. Before engaging in trading activity, you should evaluate your level of risk and trade only what you understand, otherwise it will be considered gambling. Below are some of the pros and cons associated with trading:

Pros:	Cons:
Ability to use leverage and boost profits	Leverage can be a double-edged sword, which increases lose
Velocity	Debt
Liquidity	High risk

Increased earnings	Volatility
Higher return on investment (ROI)	Could be a form of gambling for those not knowledgeable
Hedge for other investments	

For illustration purposes, there are more pros than cons. I did this because I see the positive side of trading while recognizing that negatives are involved if you do not plan accordingly. As for cons, leverage offers you the ability to increase your capital, yet it can drain your account quickly if you suffer a big loss. Using leverage is like a loan or borrowed funds that your brokerage house allows you to use for a percentage in interest. The amount of leverage can depend on factors such as your credit (Chapter 1), experience, and the financial security being traded. For instance, trading stocks will allow you to get a margin of 2:1, while foreign exchange allows a margin up to 500:1. That means that a $5,000 capital account in the foreign exchange can allow you to hold a position size up to $2.5 million while the stock market only allows you to hold up to a $10,000 position.

Do not get too excited about the foreign exchange ratio just yet, remember leverage can be a double-edged sword and could cause major financial distress if the market goes against you; greed is one of the deadliest pitfalls to a trader. A 2 percent drop in the forex market with a 500:1 margin would wipe your account out and you would be on the hook for anything above your original $5,000, if you do not exit the position in time to limit your loss.

If utilized properly, trading can act as a hedge for any investments you may have and can help offset any losses you incur through traditional investing. Ensure that you factor in the pros and cons before deciding to trade the market.

When you are trading, you are usually looking to make a profit in a short amount of time. This allows you to make quick turnarounds on any capital you have available so that you can plan for the long term through other vehicles such as stocks (Chapter 2) or real estate (Chapter 4).

You can be one of two types of traders when it comes to this market: intraday or swing trader. As an intraday trader, you trade a few times a day during one trading session in hopes of making more profit than losses; this type of trader is commonly referred to as a day trader. As a day trader financial security such as stocks, forex, and ETFs are most likely to be your best instruments to employ for trading.

A swing trader, on the other hand, is someone who buys or sells one of the financial securities that can be held for a longer timeframe. This type of trading can include stocks, options, ETFs, futures, or commodities.

Trading can be extremely profitable if you treat the market with respect and act accordingly. This area of CITRAS™ is not for the undisciplined or people who lack self-control. If you are prone to overreaction or cannot stand to see wild swings in the market, then trading is not for you; eventually this whole book may not be for you.

CITRAS™ was created to encourage you to take the necessary risks while understanding that nothing is guaranteed. My methods help to identify wealth-building tools and encourage you to investigate, mitigate, and utilize time efficient strategies. If this scares you, then I encourage you to put this book down, continue to work and live paycheck-to-paycheck, invest in your 401(K), and pay obscene amounts of taxes to the government while continuing to complain that the rich are getting richer. However, if you want to be in the same realm as the rich, then read on.

THE WONDERFUL WORLD OF TRADING

In the world of trading, the professional investors and traders earn their money by capitalizing on the way the market moves through a series of highs and lows throughout the day. This is why you typically do not see or hear about it in the news. The trading game is no different than sports; there will be winners and losers. The goal at the end of the year is to have accumulated more wins than losses.

Anyone can learn to trade the market if they learn to dispel the perceptions and background noise. I have seen testimony where a nine-year-old child learned to trade and do it profitably. If a child can do it, so can you.

Before I precede any further, I would like to ask a simple two-part question. First, have you ever played fantasy football (or any sport) or ran a league? And two, did you think it was difficult? If you have played fantasy sports and found it not to be difficult, then day trading financial securities is no different.

Imagine that a stock or whatever you are trading is a team. Each company will have its information readily available for you to view, such as upcoming products, CEO, debt, income statements, and so on. This is similar to a team's roster, salary cap, coaches, player stats, and other valuable information. Just like you would draft a player in a player versus player (PvP) league or choose one team over another in a Pick'em league, this is the same consideration you should take when choosing what security to trade.

I know some of you go all out to purchase Sports Weekly, any college or pro magazine with stats, and tune into ESPN all day long so that you are better equipped to win. Imagine putting the same effort into buying and reading *The Wall Street Journal*, *Investors Business Weekly*, economic reports, tuning into CNBC to get a read on the economy, or picking up books on investing and trading so that you can learn to hedge your investments through forex, bonds, or other securities to make quick profits through trading.

Learning to trade is more than just picking a security and taking profits. If you intend on trading, you should have a plan. You should not go into this without one. You can lose your capital in a blink of an eye if you go in wildly. The military taught me that you plan to fail if you fail to plan, so ensure that you have a written game plan for whatever security you decide to trade.

There are a few basics that you should know about and include in your plan. For instance, you should use only capital that you can afford to lose. This was mentioned earlier in the text, so you know this is an important point. Do not under any circumstance speculate in the market with your savings, mortgage, or car payment, or any other necessary funds. Also, do not use loaned funds from a bank or financial institution. In the event of a major loss, you will be deeper in a financial whole. With that being said, you should allocate your capital over many investments such as forex, stocks, options, and so on. This will help reduce the risk of a major loss and create diversification.

Trading is a game of quick decision making, so if your plan is not working then you should get out of the trade with as small of a loss as possible. Please do not try to engage in "revenge" trading after suffering a small loss or a significant loss. Revenge trading is where you try to make up for the loss by continued trading, which can lead to further losses; this will only compound the problems for you and your capital. Learn from the loss and make a new plan to mitigate it next time so that you can live to trade another day. The goal should be always capital appreciation and preservation.

Most people think that trading is a get-rich-quick scheme. In some ways it is, but most of the time it is the bigger players in the market who are getting richer quicker than you are. This is because you may not know what you are doing, you do not have as much capital as they have, or simply because they are betting in the opposite direction as you are. If you are one of those people who are looking to get rich quick, then please hand over your money to me. You will essentially be gambling, not investing or trading, if you go into the market with the goal of striking it big on either your first trade or all trades.

This is one of the reasons that people have sworn off the markets. They either do not understand the market, lost by gambling, or are afraid to enter the market because of the Great Recession. Many new investors and traders think the same thing. I had the same thoughts when I first started. I am not saying that it is impossible to strike it big, what I am saying is that it is a long shot that involves high risks and higher losses if things go awry. People strike it big almost all the time just to lose it all because of greed and overtrading.

There are many styles of traders. The main three are technical, fundamental, and hybrid. These three are typically used by beginners and professional traders alike. These styles will help you identify your strategy for trading and help you decide if intraday or swing trading is right for you. To get an understanding for them, I will briefly go over the three styles.

FUNDAMENTAL

This type of analysis is used for both trading and investing. Fundamental analysis is based on the financial strength of the company and is commonly identified by accounting ratios such as price-to-earnings ratio (PIE ratio) or by measurements such as income statements or balance sheets. Fundamental analysis can also include viewing reports from analysts or the government. Most of the information on an asset can be found fairly easy thanks to the worldwide web. Sites such as Yahoo, Moody's, and *The Wall Street Journal* offer valuable information and research on different asset classes that allows you to compare one against another. If none of these fit your criteria, then you can always visit the Securities and Exchange Commission website to gather pertinent information.

TECHNICAL

This type of analysis is typically used by traders with small accounts. Technical analysis uses charts and indicators to find trades. This type of analysis can get complicated if you allow it, so when you are trading and using the "technical" you want to focus on the price range of whatever security you are trading rather than the fundamentals. The one definition for technical analysis that I found empowering described technical analysis as "the study of how securities prices behave and how to exploit that information to make money while avoiding losses."

When trading, most traders in the game have recommended that you look at the big picture of the security by viewing it in timeframes such as one year ago, six months, one month, and current. This can then be broken down into smaller frames such as 4-hour, l-hour, and smaller. By looking at the different times in the security's life, you can establish or identify what is called a trend in the market so that you can develop lines for support and resistance; your charting should be based on your trading method whether you are trading short or long term.

Technical analysis alone is not always good; there could be something that transpired through the fundamentals that you do not know about or has not shown up on the charts, which could cause the markets to go against your position. To avoid such a catastrophe or at least mitigate it, you should consider using a hybrid method. A hybrid method is a blend of fundamental and technical analysis and is highly publicized by the market; however, you should choose the style that fits your trading goals.

HYBRID

This method is simple; it is a combination of both the fundamental and technical analysis.

This type of analysis uses fundamental information such as the PIE ratio or economic reports to decide if the security is over- or undervalue, or if it is worth buying or selling. This information is then considered with the price movement of the charts, in different timeframes, to get a gauge of the market psychology for the day or previous weeks. While using technical analysis you are still gauging and monitoring fundamental information on the security you are trading. Now that we have established how trading works, it is time to explore the first security known as options.

EVERYONE HAS OPTIONS, WHAT IS YOUR CHOICE?

The wonderful little security known as "options" is one of several ways to protect your traditional investments in stocks or can be a way to speculate and make profits.
There are multiple options available to choose from like stock options, futures options, or index options.

An option gets its value from whatever the underlying asset is, hence, why they are known as a derivative. Like all securities, options are full of advantages and disadvantages. Some of the advantages include they can be a hedge for profits already achieved, can help increase ROI, are usually purchased for a nominal fee compared to outright ownership, and can help increase income on any security that you already own. Billions of contracts are traded yearly and can indicate market sentiment if utilized properly; however, options have a disadvantage, known as an expiration date. This creates the drawback that the security cannot be held long term like stocks. The life of an option is usually a few months unless you purchase longer termed options called Long-term Equity Anticipation Securities or LEAPS for short; these contracts can be held for up to one year.

Options are derived from its underlying asset, which can be a myriad of things such as real estate, futures, ETFs, and so on. Almost anything that is tradable can be bought or sold as an option. Earlier I mentioned that one of the pros to trading was velocity, this means that the market moves up and down allowing for traders to continually profit or reuse the profits once the security is sold. The market for options is one of the most widely used financial securities because of the potential for profits.

It is important to note that an option gives you the right, but not the obligation, to purchase a position in the underlying security. This is a major plus because securities such as commodities makes you obligated to purchase to asset if you have not sold at the time of expiration or rolled over into a new contract. With an option, if you have not sold for a profit at the time of expiration then the only thing you can lose is the premium or the capital you put up for the purchase of the contract. Another awesome thing about options is that they trade for a fraction of the cost. This allows you to make a purchase based on whether you believe the asset will go up or down and make a profit without actually owning the underlying asset.

Options exist in two categories: American and European style. These options are distinctly different in that American style options can be exercised (sold) before the date it expires, while European style options can only be exercised on the date of expiration. When choosing the style of options to trade, you should consider the pros and cons of each; most options tend to trade in the American style.

Now that you know the different styles of options, I can now discuss the two types of options available for purchase, known as *calls* and *puts*. A call option is an option that gains value when the underlying security increases in value; it gives you the right to buy a certain amount of the underlying asset at a specific price before expiration. A single contract usually contains 100 shares and is commonly referred to as a "lot." If you are familiar with Christianity, then there is a mention of lots being cast for Jesus' things after he was nailed to the cross; well, this is along the same lines, at least in regard to placing a bet. Anyway, a call option will normally be noted with the letter "c," the strike price of the security, and the premium price. This will be listed under whatever security you trade, i.e., stock, future, or index.

For example, imagine that CFN Inc. is currently trading at $82.50 on the market and you decide to purchase a call option because your research concludes that the price will increase. There will be different call options available for purchase, but for this example we will say that you purchase a call for $81 with a premium of $3. This means that you will be paying $300 for the option to borrow 100 shares, or 1 contract, of CFN Inc. instead of purchasing 100 shares outright for $8,250. In order for you to make a profit, the share price will need to rise above $84, not including the purchase and selling fee.

On the other hand, a put is the opposite. With a put option, the contract gains value when the underlying security decreases in value; it also gives you the right to purchase a certain amount of the underlying asset at a specific price before expiration. A put option will normally be noted with the letter "p," the strike price of the security, and the premium. Using the previous example, we will say that this time your research concluded that CFN Inc. will drop in value because of management issues within the company. With the current price still being $82.50 you decide to purchase a put option. Various puts exist in the market, but you settle for a put with the strike price of $83 and a premium of $1.50. This means that you obtain the rights to 100 shares, or 1 contract, of CFN Inc. for $150. You will only make a profit if the shares fall below $81.50. If not, then you will only lose the $150 premium and not a larger amount, as you would if you had owned the shares outright.

Before venturing into trading securities such as options, forex, or commodities I recommend you get practice by opening an account with a brokerage firm that allows you to paper trade. Paper trading allows you to get practice with these securities without risking any real capital, so that you can test different theories without losing funds and find out what works. Find a brokerage firm that will allow you to do this and create two paper accounts; one to trade as if you were trading real money, and the other for testing various styles. This will help you prepare for when you actually do decide to use real capital.

I paper traded options with a $20,000 account and within three months I had increased my account to a value of over $40,000. I had some losses along the way, over $10,000 worth, but in the end, I made more than I lost. Paper trading will help you take the emotional part out of the equation when you win big.

Options can be a great way to increase your financial freedom, this comes from my personal experience and from the mouth of an associate who used to work on Wall Street as a trader. Now that you have a better understanding of options, I will continue with the subject at hand.

The way I remember the distinction between a *call* and a *put* is through association. For a call option I simply thought of calling someone. When you call someone, you have to pick "up" the phone and call him or her. So, a call goes up in value. With a put, I associated it with putting the phone "down"; therefore, a put goes down in value.

There are several strategies that will allow you to profit in the market whether it is a good day or bad day. The majority of these are beyond the scope of this book, such as straddles, iron condors, and strangles, but I recommend starting with the *For Dummies* series on options as a good starting point. I will go more in depth on these options in the next book. Until then, making a profit whether it is a good day or bad day will be mentioned in a later chapter, so for now commit it to memory. Also remember the fact that the financial market it based on three key areas of the economy: labor, business, and the consumer. Each area can be broken down into subsections or reports that can help you make sense of the economy. Next, I will introduce you briefly to commodities.

COMMODITIES

Commodities are in a special asset class of their own. This security can be considered an alternative investment by its own definition, but for the purpose of this book and its usefulness I will discuss trading and investing in this wonderful security. In the world of finance commodities are defined as physical goods that are grown and/or mined, then must be shipped and stored. This security can come in an assorted variety of goods such as crude oil, precious metals, and food. Entrance into this market can be done through traditional, alternative, or physical investing.

Commodities tend to increase in price due to the growth of the emerging markets sector. Countries such as Brazil, Russia, India, and China, which are known as BRIC, are growing at a higher rate than developed countries like the United States. The growth of these countries causes increased demand for commodities such as gold, silver, gasoline, metals to build cars, and food items such as bacon or soybeans. This security can help protect you when inflation is high in the producing countries, and it can mean high returns when you think of the population size of these emerging countries. Both China and India boast roughly 1 billion or more people, so the consumption of these goods will only increase the demand, which in turn will increase the price because of the limited supply.

It also helps to know what the money supply is; this can be an indicator of if commodities are rising or falling. An increase in the money supply leads to an increase in the price of commodities. Money supply refers to the increase or decrease in the currencies of the world, whether this be paper money or electronic currency. These numbers can be found on the Federal Reserve website (federalreserve.gov) or in financial sources such as *The Wall Street Journal*. This information, along with other key indicators, will give you the knowledge to invest in commodities; remember that the three key areas of the economy are useful in just about any security.

There are numerous ways to trade or invest in commodities – such as electronically – in the futures market, mutual funds, or company stocks, directly or indirectly. For example, future contracts are traded in units. The number of these units varies amongst the different types of commodities traded. Oil will come in 1,000 barrels while corn will be issued in 5,000 bushels; the number and the quality of each commodity is already preset. If this sounds a little difficult then you can always invest or trade through commodity stocks and mutual funds because they are said to be the easiest method for investing in commodities. Through this method you can purchase ETFs, stocks in commodity companies, or shares of mutual funds.

Commodities are excellent for day trading when the economy is booming. They initially lost favor during the Great Recession of 2008, yet this security is still well liked due to price movement being very easy to comprehend.

A good economy usually causes the commodity to rise, and this can continue for days and even years. For example, if the economy is strong and adding new housing starts, the need for copper and other commodities usually rises in demand.

However, there are things that can affect other commodities, like the seasons. If you have ever paid attention to the economy, you may have noticed over the years, that gasoline will rise during the summer months because of people traveling on vacation. Or you may have noticed that during the winter months, natural gas and heating oil becomes more expensive. These "cheats" are just a few commonsense notions you should keep in mind if you decide to partake in the commodities market.

Also note that this type of security typically requires large account minimums ($10,000 or more), large amounts of leverage, and should be traded between midday trading hours, i.e., 9 a.m. to 2 p.m. EST. You can start with a small account, but I recommend commodities only if you are considering trading as a fulltime gig. Now that you have been introduced to the commodities market, I would like to inform you next on the foreign exchange market or forex.

FOREIGN EXCHANGE

I mentioned in the previous section that commodities are well liked by traders. Well, when it comes to markets in general, the forex market has become the most preferred security to engage in to make a living.

In this market, rather than trading stocks, commodities, or contracts, you trade two currencies against each other. There are several currency pairs you can trade such as the Euro/U.S. dollar. This is an example of what is known in the trading world as a major currency pair. In total there are seven major currency pairs, and they constitute over 70 percent of trading volume in the forex market.

A major currency pair is when the currency of another country is paired against the U.S. dollar, and these mostly include countries of the G-7: the United States, United Kingdom, Germany, Italy, Canada, Japan, and France. The major currency pairs are as follows:

EUR/USD or Euro-U.S. dollar

USD/JPY or the U.S. dollar-Japanese yen

GBP/USD or Great Britain Pound-U.S. dollar

AUD/USD or Australian dollar-U.S. dollar

NZD/USD or New Zealand dollar-U.S. dollar

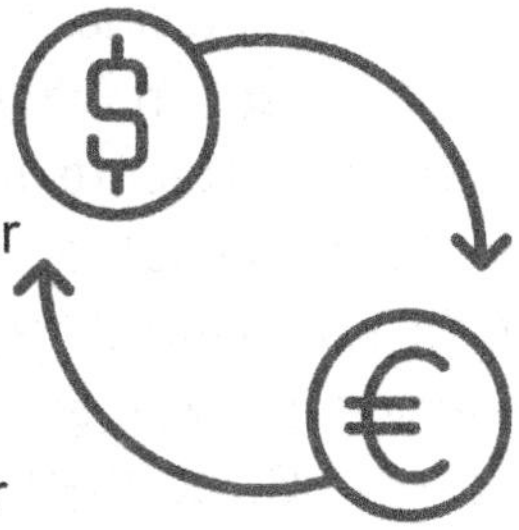

USD/CAD or U.S. dollar-Canadian dollar

USD/CHF or U.S. dollar-Swiss franc

You can trade any of these pairs on the market. This market is the largest and the most liquid of all the international financial markets. There are many people in this market, including government entities, hedge funds, and large financial institutions, all trading in minimum lot sizes of one million in base currency. These players, along with hedgers and day traders, make the market by either shorting (selling) or being long (buying) in the currency they believe will sink or rise in value.

If you will recall, I mentioned earlier that all markets are affected by the economy; well, the forex market is no different. In order to aid you in learning how to trade this security there are certain reports that you need to stay abreast of, if you want to be successful. A fundamental analysis of these reports can help you better understand the technical aspect of each currency pair.

For instance, if you want to trade any of the major pairs there are certain reports that you should look at in order to make a decision. The economics of forex is pretty simple, because if businesses are not adding jobs or supplying the market with the correct or demanded product, then the labor market will suffer. Consumers will not buy said product because either less people are working, or the supply is not what people are demanding. What I am saying is most of this is common sense.

When trading one of the major currency pairs there are several reports that can influence the greenback versus one of the other currencies. Reports that are of major significance to the U.S. dollar are labor market reports, inflation reports, gross domestic product (GDP), consumer reports, trade and current account balances, housing market sentiment, and the publishing of the Federal Reserve Beige Book, just to name a few. These reports will help you monitor and gauge the sentiment on the U.S. dollar.

Keep in mind that you should also monitor the economy of the other currency as well, *e.g.,* Europe. The reports that you should watch for in regard to the Euro are similar to the U.S. with the addition of any speeches issued by the European Central Bank (ECB), interest rate decisions, and industrial production. To get an understanding of what each area means I will briefly discuss a few of these important reports dealing with the U.S. dollar.

LABOR MARKET REPORTS

This area of the U. S. market is the primary report detailing the overall job market in the month prior. It is commonly known as non-farm payroll report or "Non-Farm Friday" because of when the report is issued. This report alone is one of the reasons that Fridays are one of the most volatile trading days. This report is composed of several main parts that include unemployment rate, average weekly hours, average hourly earnings, change in manufacturing payrolls, and change in non-farm payrolls.

Unemployment rate is important because it measures the number of unemployed individuals seeking work. An increase in this area is seen as a weakness in the labor market while a decrease is seen as a positive indicator of a strong market. At the time of this writing the unemployment rate is sitting at roughly 3.5 percent, one of the lowest in U.S. history. This, along with other factors, help contribute to your decision making in terms of deciding whether the value of the dollar will rise or fall against the currencies of other countries.

Average weekly hours will inform you as to the number of average hours worked each week. This is looked at as a gauge of business demand for labor with increased weekly hours being a positive sign for the labor market. Average hourly earnings measure any changes in employee wages and can be an indicator of consumer spending depending on if the wages are rising or falling. Once again, it all goes hand-in-hand with the economy focusing on the labor market, the consumer, and business.

Changes in non-farm payroll will tell you about the number of average jobs added each month. Conventional wisdom states that between 100,000 and 150,000 jobs need to be added to the economy in order to keep the unemployment rate steady. Market sentiment is based on the difference between the actual change and the forecasted change. If you recall in the news in the third quarter of 2019, the forecasted changes between total jobs added was said to be 500,000 lower than forecasted and it caused a ruckus in the market. Once again, that is why Fridays are so volatile.

Finally, any change in manufacturing payrolls will be a measure of jobs added or lost in the manufacturing industries and it can also help you gauge near term production activity. This, added with average hourly earnings and average weekly earnings, can give you a picture of the overall economy for the sector. As far as labor reporting goes, there are other parts to help gauge the market, but these are just a few of the major ones.

INFLATION GAUGE

This indicator helps monitor changes in the prices of goods and services. Usually, any changes in inflation to the upside will be met with higher interest rates to help offset. There are different reports to keep an eye on in this area, but some of the important ones to watch include the Consumer Price Index (CPI), the Personal Consumption Expenditure (PCE), and the Producer Price Index (PPI). The CPI is a theoretical basket of goods and services at the consumer and retail level that gauges the price we are paying. It includes items that can be used to help offset prices, especially for the military and certain businesses that issue a cost-of-living allowance (COLA). The PCE is similar to the CPI, but it is what the Federal Reserve uses as its main inflation gauge. Finally, the PPI measures change at the wholesale or producer level to see if costs are being passed along to other businesses or consumers. The PPI is said to be a leading indicator of overall inflation, so maintain your vigilance of this area.

CONSUMER REPORTS

Consumers' sort of control the markets because their psychology or sentiment is how the markets attempt to forecast future activity and the overall direction of the economy. If consumers feel good about the economy, then they will spend; however, if consumers are unsure of what the future holds, then spending slows or stops. A few key indicators to watch are the consumer confidence index and retail sales. The consumer confidence index is a monthly report that looks six months ahead and also at the present situation. For this index households are surveyed as to their opinions on the overall economic conditions, incomes, and employment. Based on the uncertainty in the trade tensions in 2019 between the U.S. and China, an impeachment hearing, the debauchery with Putin, North Korea, and "Brexit," the market was volatile, and consumers were uncertain about what the future held. This has caused the Federal Reserve to lower the interest rates to help encourage borrowing and spending so that the economy does not falter. Retail sales cover the personal spending in the U.S. for almost every purchase American consumers make. Retailers make most of their revenues during the fourth quarter, or the last three months of the year due to the holiday season and spending. Specials such as Black Friday, Cyber Monday, Christmas, and back to school shopping for the new year contributes more to the bottom-line than all the previous months. Just like commodities, weather can also have an effect on this report.

GROSS DOMESTIC PRODUCT (GDP)

GDP is a measurement of the total income activity in an economy or country over a specified period of time, usually three months. I recently learned that there are some countries that include activities such as gambling, prostitution, and the production of counterfeit goods into this number. It was said that this provides a more accurate picture of what the country is really producing and can boost GDP by 1 percent in some cases. The U.S. does not include these other activities into its measurement. Anyways, the GDP of a country is presented on an annualized term but calculated on a quarterly basis. For example, if China reports 6 percent annual growth this means that on a quarterly basis it grows at 1.5 percent (6 percent ÷ 4 quarter = 1.5 percent). You can use GDP to help compare growth amongst other countries, which can help you decide the currency that may be rising and the one falling in value.

TRADE BALANCE AND CURRENT BALANCE

Trade balance covers the difference between exports and imports. The difference will tell you if the economy is operating at a trade surplus (more exports) or at a trade deficit (more imports). A large deficit in trade or current accounts tends to lead to weaker currencies compared to countries that operate at a surplus. Current account balance details whether a country is a borrower, or a lender and it too operates at a surplus or deficit. If a country has a deficit, then it is a net borrower; if the country is at a surplus, then it is a lender.

HOUSING INDICATORS

There are at least four key pieces of information that you should look at in this area: housing starts, new home sales, existing home sales, and building permits. Not only is this information important to trading, but it is also key information for investing in real estate, which is the topic of discussion in the next chapter.

Housing starts are important because it measures the number of new home constructions that are started each month. This can be seen as a sign of housing sentiment, and it lets you know about supply and demand. If new construction is taking place, then demand is strong and can indicate a strong economy. This can lead you to the area of new home sales, which are based on an annualized account. This report counts the number of houses once the contract is signed, so if a contract gets cancelled then its numbers will be lower than originally reported. This area accounts for roughly 15 percent of all residential home sales.

Existing home sales are also reported on an annualized basis and accounts for the other 85 percent of home sales. Research shows that pending sales can be a leading indicator of existing home sales and are counted when a contract is signed to purchase an existing home. This may sound similar to new home sales, but if you look closer you notice that one is based on new home sales while the other is based on existing home sales.

New homes have to be built and that is why you need to look into the number of building permits being reported. Building permits are reported with housing starts and can be an indicator of growth. If building permits have been issued, then construction is not far behind. New construction indicates growth or expansion and is an investment in the future of the community, which will bring in employment and other businesses.

FEDERAL RESERVE BEIGE BOOK

This is an assessment complied by the twelve Federal Reserve banks and is usually issued two weeks before every Federal Open

Market Committee policy meeting. It is a summary of information based on surveys and reporting from each district's business leaders and their economics. This can help you get a handle on how the market may be developing by seeing where there are signs of inflation or what the labor market is looking like.

Now that you have a small understanding of the things that can affect the U.S. dollar compared to other currencies, it is time to learn more about the forex market. During the rest of this chapter, you will learn about some of the history of the market, advantages of forex, how to calculate profits, and top currencies to trade.

FOREIGN EXCHANGE

The foreign exchange (FX or Forex) is one of the only securities where four to five trillion dollars a day is exchanged. Can you imagine getting just a fraction of that amount on almost a daily basis? It becomes easier to do so with practice, study, and reading. The forex market is open nearly six days a week starting around noon on Sunday EST and closing on Friday; other markets are typically opened five days, excluding major holidays. You can trade currencies via online brokerages such as E*TRADE or Forex.com.

Trading the currency market is not all that new; it is almost as old as trading and bartering. The exchange of money dates back to the time of the Egyptians and can be traced to the Middle East. Trading on the market did not really happen until the 1800s. In today's age you can trade through hubs such as New York, Tokyo, Hong Kong, or Sydney just to name a few.

Everything from bank deposits to real estate goes through the forex market at one point or another; money has to be converted to the correct currency in order to bring in all the exotic cars, coffee, and seasonal fruits we all love so much. This market is so large that even the profits from credit card companies cannot compare to the forex market; this is due to the several advantages that the forex market has to offer.

Advantages of Forex

The forex has many advantages that allows for profitability. This includes speed of trading, around the clock markets, limited risk exposure, and leverage, amongst other things. Technological advances have made trading faster and more efficient than previous tools, such as using the telephone to make trades. The use of electronic platforms allows traders to make quick entries and exits into a currency pair or monitor the pair without the use of a broker.

The Internet has also made trading easier around the world; you can literally trade almost 24 hours a day in different markets because of the time zones. You can start trading at noon on Sunday EST until the closing of markets on Friday at 5 p.m. EST, which is roughly six days of trading and potentially profiting. You have limited risk exposure because of the huge volumes, few trading restrictions, and varying currency pairs so you are not limited to just one currency or currency pair. That along with the frequent buying and selling in various time frames allows for liquidity in the market. You can capture big gains in this liquid market through the use of leverage, or margin trading ratios, that can be as high as 500: 1 meaning that a deposit of $1,000 could control a position size of 500,000.

Just because the forex allows the most leverage, as high as 500: 1, does not mean that you should trade utilizing it. Do not let greed be your downfall; I have mentioned this multiple times throughout this text. You should do your homework on your trading choice so that you can make a proper decision. This is cause for learning to read charts (technical analysis) and what is going on with the security (fundamental analysis). By using both types of analysis, you can learn how to capitalize off the market whether it is going up or down. I recommend using high leverage only if you are trading tight windows for small gains such as 10-15 pips with large lot sizes.

Profiting in Forex

In order to make money trading currency, you have to determine, which currency pair will move up or down in value from the other. The pairs are said to be quoted; this explains the relationship of the currencies to one another. When you see a quoted pair, it will often contain two currency codes and a number such as EUR/USD=1.2345.

The first code is known as the base currency, which is the stronger currency of the pair and will almost always equal one. The second code is called the quote currency and is the weaker currency of the pair. In the example previously discussed, one euro is equal to $1.2345 USD. You can convert any amount from the base currency to the quote currency by multiplying the base by the quote. For instance, if you wanted to convert 50 euro to its dollar equivalent then you would multiple the base of 50 by the quoted price of 1.2345 to get $61.275.

Most currency pairs are written in the format 1/100 or 1 percent. For example, 1.2345 is the quote price for a currency pair, not to be rounded off to 1.234 or 1.235. The smallest pip, 0.0001 or 1 pip, is where you can make significant profit depending on the size of the trade. A pip or percentage in points is the movement of the currency in any direction. If the EUR/USD pair equals 1.2345 at the start of the trading session and it moves to 1.2360, then it moved 0.0015 pips or 15 points.

Interestingly, Asian currencies differ in how they are written compared to the previous example. If you see the quote for the USD/JPY pair, it will most likely read something similar to USD/JPY= 101.1234. The yen and certain other Asian currencies will seem to hold more value but recall earlier that the base currency is almost always equal to one, so 1 USD equals 101.1234 JPY in this case. This means that you receive over 100 yen in exchange for a single dollar; this is in response to actual physical value. Imagine if you are in Japan and wanted to purchase an item that costs 150 yen, you would need at least $1.50 to convert over to the yen in order to cover the cost of the item, and you would have some change left over.

Now that you understand some of the basics of what a pip is and how much it represents, I will discuss the forex market in more detail. Next, I will talk about bids, asks, and spreads, which are all fairly easy to comprehend. A bid is the price at which the trader is buying, and the market is selling; the ask is the price at which the trader is selling, and the market is buying, and the spread is the difference between the two. The asking price will always be higher than the bid.

If you are like me then you will need to see an example, so let us say that a bid price for the EUR/USD is 1.2345 and the asking price is 1.2348, what is the spread? By subtracting the bid from the ask price you notice the spread is 3 points or 0.0003 pips. The spread is what the brokers are charging you as a fee for making the market and you purchasing the pair. High volume pairs such as the EUR/USD, typically have lower spreads than lower volume pairs, which will have a high spread.

Before we get into calculating profit, it is important to understand the purchasing sizes in the forex market. You can only trade the market in certain lot sizes when it comes to making a transaction and these sizes are nano, mini, standard, and large. Each lot size constitutes a different amount in profits and losses as well as various sizes. A nano lot size is 1,000 and is worth $0.10 for each pip movement. Many online brokers do not allow such small sizes, but you can find this option if you research brokerages that offer this ability. A mini lot size is 10,000 and is worth $1, a standard lot size is 100,000 and worth $10, and a large lot size is 1 million and worth $100. You can find the value of each lot size by multiplying the size by a single pip (.0001) i.e., a standard lot of 100,000 multiplied by a pip movement of .0001 is equal to 10.

The spot market is the most traded market for the forex; this market is fast-paced and very volatile, which can lead you to get quick profits or losses. When trading in the spot markets, currencies can move in a range of 50-150 pips or more on average. With this in mind, let us say that you have been studying the market and you speculate that the U.S. dollar will decrease in value versus the Japanese yen. The quote price is currently at 106.3500 and in order to purchase a lot based on your research you need to sell the USD. Let us also say that you purchase a position size of 500,000 at the current market price and within minutes the new price is 106.3460, what is your profit?

Well, the first thing you will need to figure out is how many pips or points your position moved in your favor. To get this, you subtract your selling price (106.3460) from your purchasing price (106.3500) to get 40 points or .0040 pips. Next, you multiply your position size by the pip amount, so 500,000 times .0040 is equal to 2000. In this case you would have made a $2,000 profit.

This is only with one position size; imagine if you had purchased multiple positions at different prices that went in your favor. This however is a best-case scenario; you could have just as easily lost $2,000 or more if you did not exit your position in a timely manner or have what is known as a stop loss in place.

I know that in this section I talked a lot about the forex market, and it was by design. I know that trading the markets will work if you take the time to grasp the concept. I have a personal friend of mine who trades stocks. I have seen him turn $1,500 into $20,000 in a matter of three months. In regard to the forex market, my friend has an associate who averages $36,000 on a good day; that is the equivalent of an entry-level worker's salary made in one day!

I know people who sit at home and can pay all their bills, including a $1,500 mortgage, just by trading forex. These examples may not be how the forex market turns out for you, but it could be – if you applied yourself. Now that you have seen some positive examples of forex trading, I will now introduce you to some other pairs to consider for trading besides the old Euro-dollar pair.

TRADING CURRENCY PAIRS

As I previously mentioned, most transactions occur in the spot market. This means that trading occurs in "real time." Services for processing your trades are handled by banks like EBS or Reuter Dealing. In the spot market between four to five trillion dollars change hands, so that means there are lots of players. These transactions take place at different times at different locations.

There are some currency pairs that will trade better in the markets than others. These typically are the G-7 currency pairs that trade against the U.S. dollar. They tend to have higher trading volume, liquidity, and profit than other pairs. I am not saying that you should not trade lesser currency pairs or "crosses" (pairs that do not involve the USD).

If you can get an understanding of these other pairs and crosses, then this could be an opportunity for you; sometimes it pays to be the contrarian. Maybe you are well versed in Thailand culture or from a country like India and have firsthand knowledge of the local economy, only you can decide what is right for you.

On another note, the vast majority of trading by volume tends to take place in four major currency pairs: EUR/USD, USD/JPY,

GBP/USD, and USD/CHF. The majority of these are also considered safe haven currencies i.e., USD, CHF, and JPY. This is because people, or other countries, believe in the strength of the United States; while the Swiss franc is back by gold, has low inflation, and has a stable economy, which leads us to the yen, which has its government debt held by its own people.

Half of these transactions take place in the United Kingdom (U.K.) and the United States (U.S.) markets. London accounts for anywhere between 31-37 percent of the market while the U.S. accounts for 18-19 percent. My studies have led to the conclusion that a country and its currency tends to be most active during the opening session of its market such as the euro at the London open. To conclude this chapter, I will discuss each major dollar pair and some important information you should know about each one.

EUR/USD

This pair is the most actively traded pair in the forex; it seems like anyone who trades currency is in this market. This pair does not have any nicknames like other pairs; however, when you are conducting research, you should understand whether an analyst or writer is referring to a currency pair or the individual currency.

For example, the "Swissy" refers to the USD/CHF pair together, so if an analyst stated the Swiss franc was falling in value due to trade tensions this would only refer to the individual currency, not the pair as a whole. In the EUR/USD pair the dollar is pitted against the whole Eurozone. The entire Eurozone is roughly equal to the U.S. in terms of GDP and size. In the pair, the euro is the base currency, and the dollar is the quote currency. The euro may be stronger, but the dollar is the world currency.

When trading this pair, you need to know which currency is carrying the pair. This pair is said to trade inversely to the overall value of the dollar. What that means is that if the pair goes up, then the euro is getting stronger, and the dollar is getting weaker. In this case it takes more dollars to make one euro. On the other hand, if the pair is going down then the euro is getting weaker, and the dollar is getting stronger. In other words, you would sell the pair if you thought the dollar was improving as it was during late 2019. On the other hand, you would buy if you thought the dollar was declining.

Trading online is the most significant way to enter the forex market. When trading the EUR/USD, there are certain things you should know about it. First, the pair is traded in amounts that are denominated in euros, so a standard lot size would be €100,000. Just for general information, a currency pair will be denominated in the base currency. Secondly, even though the pair is denominated in euros the profits and losses accrue in dollars, so a one-point change in a standard lot is a $10 gain or loss depending on your position. Finally, your margin calculations for online platforms will also be denominated in dollars. During the time of this writing the EUR/USD was trading at 1.0975, so if you wanted to trade a single standard lot on a 100:1 margin it would cost you $1,097.50. The higher the pair trades, the more margin is required, and vice versa.

Keeping abreast of both currencies and their respective economy will be important in speculating the directional movement. For instance, if your research shows that U.S. economic data is weak then you should look to sell the dollar against other currencies, mainly the euro in this case. This is why you need to know which currency is driving the direction and, what the market is saying in terms of reports and events. In short, the overall tendency of the pair to move is based on U.S. data and news; however, Eurozone reporting can also cause the pair to move.

USD/JPY

The yen is the third most traded currency in the world after the euro and dollar. This currency is said to trade around the clock and has the second largest national economy in terms of GDP. Just like the EUR/USD, this pair does not go by a nickname. When dealing with this pair, the dollar is the base currency, and the yen is the quote currency. It was trading at roughly 186.28 during this writing in 2019. Some basic fundamentals of the USD/JPY include the pair trading in the same direction as the overall value of the dollar and inversely to the yen. This means that if the dollar is strengthening while the yen is getting weaker, then the pair will move higher. And if the dollar is weakening while the yen is gaining strength, then the pair will move lower. This is what happened during the third quarter of 2019 when the dollar was down roughly three percent compared to the yen.

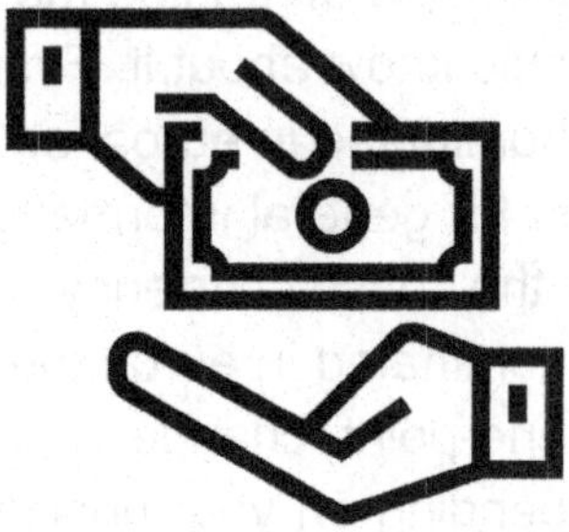

In online trading, there are fundamentals you should know about this pair. First, the pair is traded in denominations of dollars. This means that a standard lot size is 100,000 unlike the EUR/USD where a standard lot is €100,000. Secondly, your profits and losses are measured in yen, so profits and losses need to be converted.

For example, to convert U.S. dollars to Japanese yen, you divide the yen amount by the USD/JPY rate, If the amount is 106.28, then 1000 yen is equal to $9.41 (1000/1 06.28). The platform you are trading on will automatically convert your profits and losses into the proper currency, but this is information that can be useful to know.

Finally, any margins will be calculated in USD, so you can easily figure out how much you need to hold a position. At a 100:1 margin you would need $1,000 to hold a standard lot size. This can be found by dividing the size (100,000) by the leverage (100) to get the margin required, which is 1,000. This will only work with straightforward calculations where the USD is the base currency.

Be careful about trading this pair, it is politically sensitive. The Japanese officials will not hesitate to influence the pair through some form of intervention. The Japanese financial press devotes serious attention to their currency in the same manner that the U.S. does with the Dow Jones Industrial Average (DJIA) or the Standard & Poor's 500 (S&P 500). Intervention by Japan can be either verbal or through large market orders that help to push the yen in the direction the officials want. When trading the USD/JPY, you should focus on the key reports coming out of both countries. The main Japanese reports you should focus on include bank lending, industrial production, machine orders, and any reports similar to the U.S. such as the CPI, trade balance, or any major decisions.

GBP/USD

This major dollar pair is commonly known as sterling or cable. This is the first pair within the major pairs that has one or more nicknames. The liquidity and trading volume of this pair is significantly less than the previously mentioned pairs and tends to have trading similarities to the USD/CHF (U.S. dollar and Swiss franc). Most pound transactions take place on the London Exchange. If you recall earlier, I mentioned that most countries and its currency trade better in its opening session. The pound is said to be heavily traded against the euro and the dollar, but less so against all other currencies. It can be heavily influenced by cross-border trades and mergers and acquisitions (M&A) between the U.K. and Europe; however, with Brexit close at hand the pound may continue to be volatile for a while.

Trading for the GBP/USD pair is denominated in pounds. By now I assume you have an understanding of how currencies work and the denominations, but I will continue to explain so that is will be clear. When trading this pair, your profits and losses will accrue in dollars, so a standard lot position size will equal $10 per pip. This means that your margins will also be calculated in terms of dollars, so if the quote price is 1.208 then a standard lost cost $1,208 in available capital at 100:1 margin. To calculate this, you multiply the quote rate by the size then divided by the leverage:

Quote x Size = 1.208 x 100,000 = $1,208
Leverage = 100

The good thing about the GBP/USD pair is that it trades alongside the EUR/USD. This means that it moves inversely to the overall USD, so if the news in the U.S. is weak then both the GBP/USD and EUR/USD will both move higher with the GBP/USD rallying more! The volume for this pair will usually peak during the UK/Eurozone trading session and starts to diminish during the New York afternoon session, so you should look to trade at the most advantageous time. U.K. news affects this pair more than U.S. local news would when compared to the EUR/USD pair, so keeping informed of key data reports is highly important.

USD/CHF

This pair used to consider the Swiss franc a safe haven currency back during the Cold War era. This is no longer the case, but many people still refer to it as one. This is because the franc is said to closely resemble the strength and quality of the economy and finance.

Switzerland is a relatively small country with no dangerous political exposure, it has a close economic relationship with the Eurozone, it is a neutral country, and it has a good reputation for its banking services. The USD/CHF is known by its nickname of "Swissy" and traders tend to buy this pair in response to geopolitical risk or on acts of terrorism, which there has been a lot of during 2019. This pair is purchased more out of panic than because of it being a safe haven that it once was.

The overall direction of this pair follows the dollar, so if the dollar is strengthening, then the pair will move higher and vice versa. As far as the lot sizes, they are denominated in the terms of dollars. With your understanding of how other pairs work, you should know that any profits or losses will accrue in franc. So, if the quote for the pair is 1. 0125, then 10 francs equals $9.87 USD. Your pip value will change over time as the level of this pair fluctuates. As far as margins go, this one is straightforward much like the USD/JPY, meaning $1,000 is needed for a standard lot at a margin of 100:1.

When trading the USD/CHF, it is important to keep abreast of what is happening in the Eurozone. This is due to the point that Switzerland conducts the majority of its foreign trade with the European Union and other Eurozone countries. You should also monitor the following Swiss data when deciding to trade this pair: trade balance, unemployment rate, CPI and PPI, Swiss National Bank speeches or decisions, as well as retail sales. You may have noticed a pattern in the information you will need to watch for each individual country is similar if not the same.

This will help you to gather information quickly and skim over the nonessential data. When trading this particular pair, you need to be able to make quick decisions because liquidity is low and extremely volatile, which can lead to quick profits or losses.

Now that you have been introduced to the wonderful world of trading and the different ways to get into this market, you can start building your way to financial success through this option. If you trade properly and make more profits than losses, then you could use the funds to further expand your wealth or success by venturing into out next method, which is real estate.

4

REAL ESTATE

I once read a quote that has stuck with me: "Success is like a recipe. If you use the same ingredients and follow the same step-by-step instructions, you will create the same results, like anyone else." I have found this to be true when it comes to success in real estate. People have become financially successful for years in the real estate market by following the same steps as other investors.

Real estate provides multiple benefits that will allow you to be financially independent. For instance, it can provide you with a continuous monthly income source, a "cash flow," especially if you own multiple units. It can be a safety net in hard times and better than any life insurance policy. It can take care of your family long after you have passed away, if your finances are properly organized.

This type of investment alone has made more people millionaire, multimillionaires, and even billionaires per capita than any other investment. Most newly made wealth, roughly 90 percent, has been shown to be made in the real estate market.

The earth's population is steadily increasing, yet the land on which to build stays the same. In economics, the theory of supply and demand points out that over time an increase in demand with a limited supply will result in an increase in value. That is partly how the real estate market works and why having rental properties or income-producing properties will make you money. Getting into real estate can be done in several ways. You can invest in:

- Single family homes
- Multifamily apartments
- Commercial buildings
- Duplex, Triplex, and Quads Retail
- Mixed use buildings
- Mobile homes
- Undeveloped or developed land
- Storage units
- Wholesale, leasing, options, etc.

These are just a few of the way you can start to profit from owning some sort of real property.

Unlike trading and investing, real estate is different because all the control is in your hands. *You* get to make the decisions that control your future, not some boring chart or market sentiment that changes with people's mood. Real estate also provides you with several other advantages that being an employee, trader, or business owner does not. With real estate you are protected from inflation. You can use leverage (OPM) to buy rental property, and then let the property pay for itself through rent collected from your tenants. Also compounding your benefits is the fact that profits can be realized in multiple ways, like cash flow, tax benefits, appreciation, depreciation, and benefits of use.

Some of you may be thinking that real estate might not be for you or that it sounds too good to be true. You may not want to deal with tenants, maintenance issues, or you just do not have the money. Well, there are solutions to all your problems.

If you own enough properties and they generate sufficient income, then you can outsource to a property management company that will deal with the tenants and maintenance issues for a small percentage of your revenue; this will allow you to sit back and collect "mailbox" money.

The point about not having the money can be easily fixed by having a little creativity as well as using banks, family and friends, investors, or any crowd funding site. The possibilities are infinite if you are hungry enough to get a deal done. If not, then you can learn to wholesale real estate. If you want to know what that entails, I recommend checking into books by Todd Fleming. The information I obtained from him is very practical and easy for anyone to understand, whether you are a beginner or professional.

Even with the information I have listed, real estate may not be for everyone. The negatives to owning property may scare some of you off: negative cash flow, illiquidity, safety and personal liability, and management issues. Just like any other problem in life these too can be mitigated.

A property with a negative cash flow problem means that you are coming out of pocket each month to cover expenses instead of the rent covering the principal, interest, taxes, and insurance. It's a *money pit!* A simple fix for this is to increase the income (*e.g.,* raise the rents) or lower your expenses (*e.g.,* conserve energy). Even if the problem of negative cash flow still exists after increasing income or lowering expense, you can offset the loss at tax time to help reduce or even eliminate any loss suffered throughout the year!

As far as liquidity goes, you should not get into real estate if you are looking for liquidity, which refers to the ability to convert an asset to cash quickly. Real estate takes time to sell, so this makes for a longer convertibility in terms of seeking cash. If you are really in need of liquidity, you could sell at a steep discount; however, this should not be the purpose for you investing in real estate to begin with.

Safety and personal liability can both be negated by discussing your situation with a real estate attorney. A real estate attorney will help you navigate the intricacies of the real estate investment world and set up plans to help lower your risk. This could include setting up a corporate structure such as a limited liability company (LLC) or corporation. Either of these structures will allow you protection in the event something happens, such as a slip and fall, and your tenant decides to sue you. Your personal property will be protected and only the business is liable for any judgment that may occur, as long as you ran your business as a business and not like a personal bank. As far as management goes – as I mentioned before – you can outsource to a good property management company and only collect checks.

Real estate is by far one of the safest investments around, and it has only gotten easier with the development of software, the Internet, and experienced real estate investors who are willing to share information. I know I am giving praise to real estate as if it's the best thing since sliced bread. That's because I want you to be just as excited about building your way to wealth and freedom as I am.

The question you have to ask yourself when it comes to real estate investing is why you want to be in business for yourself. In order to be successful, you will have to have a work ethic, be responsible, have the ability to solve problems or at least be resourceful, and you have to want to serve others because you will be in the service industry.

I decided that real estate was right for me because I enjoy the sense of ownership. It was also a way for me to leave a legacy, and I was tired of living paycheck-to-paycheck while depending on "job security" in the military. I decided it was time to take charge of my own life, so I got educated, and now I am passing on my knowledge to you.

When dealing with real estate you are mainly dealing with two types: residential and commercial real estate. Residential properties include anything people can live in such as condos, apartments, or single-family homes. It really consists of everything that puts a roof over your head while you sleep at night. Commercial real estate, on the other hand, deals with places where someone does business, like warehouses, office buildings, or retail spaces. This type of real estate can be cyclical in nature and depends too much on the economy, major financing, and other factors. So, for the purpose of this book, I will stick strictly to residential properties and how you can learn to profit from them.

GETTING STARTED IN REAL ESTATE

I am sticking to residential properties for several reasons: 1) everyone needs somewhere to live, so you can easily buy or sell; 2) understanding the market is easier; 3) residential properties are easier to purchase than commercial, and 4) it can also act as a place for you to live. To get started in real estate and prosper, you need to learn how to lower your risk and maximize your profits. This can be done by learning how to read the market, utilizing an appropriate strategy, and thinking outside the box.

Reading the Market

Learning how to read the market in real estate is similar to using fundamental and technical analysis for investing and trading. You are using the fundamentals of economics to grasp what is going on in the real estate market in order to gauge what strategy to use. Secondly, you are using technical analysis by looking at any analytics the market may offer, such as growth rate in your area on a year over year basis or charts from your local Chamber of Commerce showing paths of growth.

To get a read on the market, you need to know the business cycle the market is in so you can apply a strategy. There are four types of markets you should be familiar with when dealing with real estate: up markets, down markets, peak markets, and bottom markets. These markets are relatively simple and can help you understand what will work best in each.

An up market informs you that prices in the market are rising; this is called a seller's market, meaning that there are more buyers than sellers. The demand is greater than supply, which creates upward pressure on prices. This is usually a good time to exit the market or sell for a profit if you are looking to do so.

A down market is the opposite. In a down market, prices are dropping because of an oversupply in the market with less demand. This is most likely a good time to look at buying or expanding your holdings because the market is reaching saturation and there will be motivated sellers looking to offload property. In effect, this is known as a buyer's market because more people are looking to sell than to buy.

In a peak market, prices have reached their maximum point thereby creating what is known as a bubble. Prices are high during this time and are about to start heading downward. Usually buyers and sellers equal out, which may cause prices to drop; this is effectively known as a bubble market.

Once a bubble is reached and prices start to drop a bottom market is the result. This is where prices have reached their lowest point and the supply and demand is equal again. Once this happens then the cycle will start over. This is why real estate is so exciting; it is because money can be made short or long term in any market cycle.

Knowing what cycle the market is in can assist you in developing an appropriate strategy, but you must also be aware of factors such as demographics and economic indicators that reveal if an area is worth investing in or not. It is advised that you should start investing locally when getting your feet wet in real estate. You should know the area in a way that an outside investor cannot, you have firsthand knowledge, and if any problems arise with your property, you are in the immediate area.

I personally believe that if you have done your homework and an area outside of your immediate area is more profitable, then you should go for it, especially if you can put together a team to handle operations. This may be a little advanced for some, but as I have been saying throughout this book, you should choose what is right for you.

Some key indicators that you will need to evaluate when you are looking to invest are demographics, psychographics, building permits, household size, employment, and market rates for rentals in the area. These indicators will help you better identify the areas in your city or any area that has the strongest markets. They can also help you see where the market is headed so that you can act ahead of the trend. Knowing your demographics helps you determine who will rent from you. This information can be found via the Census Bureau or by using a Google search for the local zip code. Demographic information will give you pertinent information such as gender, income, education level, and average household size. By viewing all of this information, you can find out if the population is growing or shrinking. It also helps you determine what your audience wants.

This is where amenities such as a close proximity to shopping centers, great school district, or pools come into play; this is known as psychographic information. Knowing your customer base and what they want in advance will help dramatically reduce any vacancies in your properties.

Building permits help you track growth. By knowing the number of permits pulled, where and when the building is scheduled, and the type of building being built, you can learn the path of growth. The local government agency will issue these permits before building is scheduled to begin, so knowing this information gives you an idea of supply and demand.

Usually permits are pulled for things such as office space, single-family homes, apartments, and retail spaces. This will bring in new businesses as well as employment, which is another indicator. Anytime employment is strong in an area there will be a need for housing. Employment will also be a key indicator to your demographic. You can find this type of information and more by checking with your local county commission office, the Census Bureau, or through Google search.

When it comes to purchasing real estate, you would not want to own multiple holdings with one bedroom and one bathroom if your local demographic has an average household of 3.5 persons. Knowing the average household size will allow you to purchase the proper mix of units. If the local area has an average of 3.5 persons per household, your mix should at least have two bedrooms and two bathrooms or better. This will help you rent out your property instead of being vacant and spending unnecessary funds on useless advertising. This is another area of research that can be found in reports from the Census Bureau.

Knowing the market rate for rentals is important in helping you understand the price range you can charge your tenants for rent. It is also a forward-looking tool if you utilize it properly. Sites like Padzing or even using Google can help aid you in finding historical and present rates. This information will help you identify if rates are increasing year over year, decreasing, or staying the same. You can also use this to forecast if your cash flow will improve or will you give a diminished return on your investment because the particular market you are looking at is stagnant and interest is eating away at your profits.

By understanding key indicators and understanding the market, you can then decide on what strategy to use. This should be thought out well in advance of purchasing the property; it is what is known as "beginning with the end in mind" or strategic planning. If you have read any type of real estate literature, you will find that most investors agree there are three types of strategies being used. One of these strategies is heavily showcased on television, in written media, and broadcasted on radio while the other two sits in the background. The three types of strategies that

you can utilize once you have conducted your research are the fix and flip, the long-term keeper, and the short hold.

Strategies

Fix and Flip

The fix and flip style strategy have been the current trend for roughly ten years in the real estate market. The goal of this strategy is to purchase property, fix it up, and sell it for quick profits. These properties are occasionally found through foreclosure, tax sales, auctions, or through desperate homeowners. You can also look for distressed properties that are in poor condition or in need of major repair, like the one I mentioned as my missed opportunity. This can be a good strategy in a hot market; however, because fix and flip is thinking short term it will not be considered passive income.

These projects are typically held less than a year, therefore they are considered and taxed as ordinary income, meaning that if your personal income is taxed at 35 percent then so are your profits from flipping properties. Add this to the fact that you may need or require large working capital; your profits may be lower than expected. Many new investors tend to employ this strategy to gain financial breathing room, especially if they own other types of property.

When deciding to fix and flip properties, you need to consider remodeling costs, any holding costs of the property if it is not immediately sold after the fix, your worst-case scenario (*e.g.,* becoming a landlord or drop in home value), as well as trends in the market. If you do decide to pursue this strategy, then it is recommended that you use the following equation to evaluate your potential property:

Sale cost + Holding cost + $2 for every $1 of repairs + labor at current trade rate + 10 percent markup = Sales price

This will help you see if the project is worth pursuing or if it is a bust. There are sources out there to help aid you if you want to employ this strategy. One source that I came across is CapStone Lending. This business is rated 5 stars and they will lend or fund your projects. They offer 100 percent of purchase/rehab price, 80 percent of as-is value, or 70 percent of after-rehab value.

Long-term Keeper

The long-term keeper does not necessarily mean you have to hold it forever. With a long-term keeper you are looking to keep the property with the goal of the mortgage being paid off from the rental income so that you own the property free and clear of any liens. These types of properties are usually located in neighborhoods that are less likely to decline in value and are fairly easy to rent. The long-term keeper can be held to generate cash flow, for appreciation, or for the additional capital you can build through equity.

If you finance this type of property with the goal of holding, then you should utilize a fixed interest rate if you use traditional sources of financing, such as a bank. You can find properties like this in more affluent or upscale areas that provide a multitude of amenities (think psychographics). People will pay for comfort of ease, so if you make things such as shopping or dining out easier, then most people will think the price is worth it.

Short Hold

The short hold strategy should likely be applied to property that is in the low to middle price range. Apply this strategy with properties you want to hold for one to three years with the goal that it will appreciate enough to sell at a higher price. This is a great strategy to use for the Millennial generation who are currently looking for affordable homes.

These properties are easy to either rent or sell; most of the time they will provide great cash flow as well. Investors who employ this strategy buy these types of properties during the down cycle and sell when the market it up; it is like purchasing quality stock when the stock markets are down and people are panicking, when you know that the markets will eventually rise in price again.

You should ultimately choose a strategy that works for you. I believe that a mixture of all three strategies is the way to build real lasting wealth and financial success; it is no different from using a combination of technical and fundamental analysis when investing or trading securities.

When I look at these strategies, I think of them in the form of an analogy. I love to make money and I love to eat, so I compare the two. I view long-term keepers as the main course meal with steak, potatoes, asparagus, and good wine; this is because a keeper pays for itself and keeps you and your family "full." A short hold is like an appetizer, it holds you until the main course arrives, which you get after selling the property in an up market. If you think about it, this is a combination of a keeper and a flip.

Finally, we have dessert, which is your fix and flip property. You do not want too much dessert, but it is good to have some every now and then. A fix and flip is for quick profits so you can move on to better properties or to have some breathing room if other properties are lagging. Now that you have an understanding of how to read the market and different strategies you can employ, let's look at ways you can finance your properties.

FINANCING REAL ESTATE

There are three steps to purchasing real estate: 1) find a property to buy, 2) negotiate a price with the seller, and 3) find cash or some sort of financing to pay the seller so you can take ownership. When it comes to finding cash to purchase the property, most people initially look to the traditional sources of financing such as banks, mortgage companies, or mortgage brokers.

There are other forms of traditional financing that you may not be aware of, especially when dealing with rental properties. Financing can be pursued through insurance companies, pension funds, or your own 401(K). When it comes to investing in real estate, you should be looking at these forms as well as other sources of financing.

Thinking outside the box will carry you a long way in the real estate business. Financing by using hard money loans, seller financing, state loans, or other creative forms of financing can help you close deals. Who knows, maybe even a combination of different financing methods may be the answer to ownership. Whatever you need to do to get the deal done should be considered, as long as it makes economic sense and is legal.

Traditional Financing

Back in chapter one I talked about credit and the benefits it will bring you in creating financial success, well this is the time it can come in and play one of its most important roles. Using traditional sources of finance will likely have you and your credit under scrutiny, so if you skipped chapter one or casually thumbed through it, then go back and check it out. Other than that, let us get into more details dealing with traditional financing methods.

Mortgage Companies

This source of financing is the largest as far as lending goes. You can literally find thousands of these through an Internet search or catch a few television advertisements from Lending Tree or Rocket Mortgage. These companies originate their own loans using their own funds. Money for them is made by creating these loans and charging you fees.

They also resell packaged loans to banks, government service enterprises (GSEs), or pension funds as mortgage-backed securities (MBS) or asset-backed securities (ABS). By doing so, these companies can make more loans without keeping their funds tied up in long-term mortgages. Before choosing a company, due to there being so many, it is best to comparison shop for the best deal; you would not want to pay a premium to borrow money if you do not have to, as it will eat away at your own profits.

Mortgage Brokers

These people are not lenders but intermediaries who match borrowers and lenders together. If you work with a broker, they will tend to have several lenders and will look to find you the best deals. In a sense, mortgage brokers deal in loans that other lenders may not, such as people with not-so-decent credit.

The networks of lenders that mortgage brokers work with are most likely private lenders, and the loans will come at high costs and high interest rates to you. This method allows you to see once again why credit is important to wealth building.

On the chance that you decide to use a broker, you should interview this person before deciding to work with him or her. Find out how many different banks or lenders he or she works with, how long has this person been in business, what are the charges for origination and application fees, along with other high-end questions. You should think of this as if you are looking to fund your real estate business and this is your chance to interview and possibly hire a potential employee. Maybe this will be a one-time transaction, or it could turn into a lifetime partnership; either way, you have to ask the tough questions.

Banks

Before approaching this avenue and possibly lowering your credit score, you should look into getting prequalified. By prequalifying for a loan, you will eliminate having to go through the rigorous process of searching for a loan and possibly getting denied.

A prequalification or "prequel" lets you know in advance what amount the bank will likely loan you based on information you provided. Banks like to make short-term, high-interest loans but are known for making these longer termed loans for real estate. Looking for bank financing can be done at your large financial institutions like Wells Fargo, or you can go with a credit union or savings and loan (S&L) bank.

One of the secrets to building wealth is using other people's money or OPM. By getting financing from banks, you are leveraging your investment – in the same manner as you would in trading or investing in the securities market – to increase your profit margin and lower your risk.

Once you get prequalified for financing, your loan can be structured in a variety of ways. There are a multitude of books and information on the Internet dedicated to this subject, so I will not overwhelm you with loan structures. For the purpose of this book, I will only discuss three of the most common types of loans: Fixed rate, adjustable-rate mortgage (ARM), and interest only loans.

When taking out a loan for property, you should consider the elements of principal, interest, and time. They are the sources that make what is known as your mortgage payments. The key to understanding your payment schedule is that the more you borrow, the higher your payments will be, the longer the period, the lower the payments. Finally, a high interest rate leads to higher payments; it seems common sense, right?

Fixed Rate Mortgages

Fixed rate mortgages can come in various shapes and sizes, but the two most common types are the 15-year and the 30-year mortgage. With a fixed rate mortgage your payment will not change for the entire life of the loan. It is the same as getting a car loan with equal payments for five years or more.

You are amortizing the loan, which means that at the end of whatever the term is the loan will be completely paid off. Fixed rate mortgages are easy to understand so there will be no surprises down the line as to what you will be paying, unlike other loan forms such as adjustable-rate mortgages.

The shorter the period, the higher your mortgage payment will be. This is not always a bad thing, considering a longer period means you will end up paying more interest even though your payment will be lower. A shorter period can be justified if the income from the property can support it.

If you would like to figure out monthly mortgage payments, there are financial calculators that perform this function, or you can Google "mortgage calculator" then enter all the known information. To see the difference between a 15-year mortgage and a 30-year mortgage I will go through an example.

Let us say that you want to find out the monthly mortgage payment to amortize $300,000 at 5 percent for 30 years. Based on the mortgage calculation chart, the monthly payment for a 30-year loan $1,610.46. Before I continue, I would like to say that as an investor it is important that you have a mortgage calculation chart or calculator so that you can do estimations on possible investment properties to see if it makes financial sense.

Now that I have gotten that out of my system we can continue. With the payments figured out for a 30-year mortgage, you now decide to run the numbers on a 15-year mortgage to see if it would be better, so you plug in the known information, and it reads a monthly payment of $2,372.38. A 15-year mortgage adds a whopping $761.92 to your monthly payments!

This may seem like a lot of money but let us look at this from a broader perspective. The 30-year loan has a monthly payment of $1,610.46, which equates to $19,325.52 on an annual basis, so in 30-years you end up paying a total of $579,765.60 to borrow $300,000. That means you paid $279,765.60 in interest, over *90 percent* in loan value – you almost paid back double what you borrowed!

Now let us look at the 15-year loan with a monthly payment of $2,372.38 or $28,468.56 in annual payments. In 15 years, you end up paying $427,038.40 for a $300,000 loan, which totals only $127,028.40 or 42.3 percent interest in loan value. You save $152,737.20 or $10,182.48 annually by going with a 15-year mortgage. This is money you could save or use to invest in another property.

This example gives you a general idea, with a comparative rate. The take-away is a 15-year loan is cheaper than a 30-year loan, and in the real-world the 15-year loan will also have a lower rate. So, if you expected to pay 5 percent for a 30-year loan, you could reasonably expect to pay at least a half percent lower for a 15-year loan, or 4.5 percent.

Long-term loans are designated for properties that you intend to hold or use the profits to boost or improve the property. Fixed rate loans allow for more stability than other types of loans, which means that if interest rates drop you will not benefit but if they rise then you are protected from inflation. This is why adjustable-rate mortgages, or ARMs, will be discussed next.

Before I move on, I would like to leave you with some extra knowledge on fixed loans. If the loan allows you to pay more than the loan payment, then send in extra payments towards the principal. When you do, ensure that your lender knows that the payment should be applied to the principal or they may consider it an early payment, which won't benefit you nearly as much.

Adjustable-Rate Mortgage

ARMs have become almost as common as fixed rate loans for investors and home buyers. These loans have variable interest rates, meaning that the interest you are paying year to year will change.

ARMs have predetermined minimums and maximums known as "caps" and "floors" that state the highest and lowest your rate can adjust over the life of the loan. They can also have built in periodic adjustments called "collars" where the rate will not adjust more than a certain amount, such as 2 percent annually or as defined by the loan. These rates are typically linked to either a treasury rate, prime rate, or some sort of index interest rate.

Most banks like these types of mortgages because it gives them protection in the event that rates rise, unlike when servicing a fixed rate mortgage. The most common ARMs will adjust in one of three ways: monthly, biannually, or as a hybrid. With monthly ARMs the interest rate is recalculated monthly, so your payments may be higher or lower depending on what the rate is. Biannual adjustments happen every six months and hybrid loans are truly variable in their structure.

In the beginning a hybrid ARM is fixed for a certain amount of time, which can range from one year to ten years, then adjusts annually after the initial period has expired. For example, you can get a 7/1 ARM, meaning that your rate will be fixed for the first seven years and will adjust every year after that.

ARMs make great economic sense if you plan on holding the property for less than five years, *i.e.,* short hold properties. You should look into working with an experienced broker if you decide to go this way. ARMs are also great if you know that rates will lower, if you intend to sell in a few years, or if cash flow can support the variable payments.

I suggest using this structure if your property will experience significant appreciation during the fixed-rate period and you are using a short hold strategy. This will allow you to benefit from greater cash flow and to profit from the appreciation once the property is sold. You can look to the Federal Reserve for information forecasting whether rate will rise or fall, so that you can make a decision if an ARM is right for the property you are pursuing. Next on the agenda is interest-only loan.

Interest-Only Loans

This loan structure has everything in its name; you are only paying interest on the mortgage. Usually this can be as short as three years, but it can also stretch to as long as ten years, similar to ARMs. With an interest-only loan, you are paying nothing towards the principal (the amount borrowed), so if you took out a loan for $300,000 you will still owe that amount plus interest after the initial time period expires. After that, you can pay the increased amount, sell the property to pay off the loan, or refinance the property.

An interest-only loan allows for greater cash flow so that you can improve the property through forced appreciation or double up by keeping the profits and waiting it out while the property appreciates on its own.

Using this loan structure does have its negative points. You may not be able to refinance the property in a difficult market and you will not be paying down the principal. So, if you make interest payments for three years on a $300,000 loan, you will still owe $300,000 plus interest at the end of those three years; there is no amortizing with this structure. You could also end up having a balloon payment at the end of the term, meaning that you have to pay the whole amount in full or you will default on the loan.

Ensure that you know what you want to do with the property before getting financing. Having an exit plan will allow you to understand what type of financing will best serve you. For example, if you intend on flipping properties then a variable rate mortgage is most likely the best way to go. This is because you intend to sell quickly, and interest rates are usually lower in the beginning phase. This could protect you in the case you become an "accidental landlord." On the other hand, an investor who intends to make a property a keeper should look into fixed rate mortgages or hybrid ARMs, like a 7/1 to help increase cash flow; however, if you discern that rate will increase then stick with fixed rates only.

Traditional financing is an excellent way to go if you can afford it; however, there are those of us who may not have the stellar credit rating to be approved for good traditional financing. This is where thinking outside the box can be of service to you. Learning to finance real estate deals outside of traditional financing is what is known as "creative financing." People use this type of financing regardless of whether they can afford to use traditional methods or not.

A mile-long list can be created that shows you ways that people have found or created in order to generate real estate deals and build their way to financial success. In the next section I will detail three creative ways investors have financed deals. The three ways that will be discussed are seller carryback financing, assumption of mortgage, and seller carried second mortgage.

CREATIVE FINANCING

Seller Carryback Financing

This can be the easiest way to finance a property if the seller owns the property outright. Seller carryback financing is commonly known in the real estate industry as "seller financing," and it can be done quite simply. Seller financing involves two people agreeing on a rate of interest, terms and conditions, drawing up the necessary paperwork, and closing the deal. This is an excellent way to go, even if you can get financing from an institutional lender.

Seller financing can create a win-win for both parties if structured properly. It can allow the seller to receive full asking price (which is rare), still receive income, and avoid costly fees while being able to receive ownership back in the event of default. For the buyer, advantages can include having to put no money down, great interest rate on the loan, and receive rights to the income of the property. It also gives you a chance as the buyer to build up a cash reserve so that you can either refinance with an institutional lender or sell at a higher price in the future. You will need to build the seller's trust in you or find a desperate seller in order to getting to finance this good.

Seller financing usually works better in a slow market because there are not as many buyers, and the seller may be looking to unload the property, however, this can still work in an up market if you can make a convincing declaration to the seller. When looking to a seller for financing, it is important that you showcase the benefits of this person providing you seller financing and not just as a way to get rid of the property. You should highlight that by offering you financing he or she will receive a better rate of interest than placing the money into a bond, savings account, or certificate of deposit (CD).

Also, this person will get more cash back from the sale of the property than initially invested, thus giving him or her a greater return on investment. Do not forget to mention that if the money is not needed right away or if the person is looking to retire, then any payments received from you for mortgage payments will be like receiving an annuity for as long as the period you all agreed upon. Plus, all profits are secured by the property itself, which means that this person has security in getting paid. The seller essentially becomes the bank and gets to keep all the profits while earning a steady rate of interest. If this does not convince the seller to provide you financing then you can always try the next method of creative financing, which is assuming the mortgage.

Assumption of Mortgage

Assuming the mortgage is another wonderful way to gain control of real estate. You can try using this method if the seller may be facing foreclosure or just wants to get out of the property. You benefit from this method because it will allow you to conserve any cash you may have, which leaves you with some working capital. This can also benefit both parties if the seller has an assumable loan that does not trigger a "due-on-sale" clause.

An assumable loan can be an approach to use if the interest rates have risen and the current rate on the loan is lower; however, these types of loans are rare because lenders will want to either raise the interest rate or call the loan, which triggers the due-on-sale clause. On the other hand, even if you can assume the loan, the seller may be the one wanting a higher price in order for you to assume the loan because the loan may only cover a small portion of the cost; this can be overcome by having the seller take out a second mortgage as part of the purchase price.

Seller Carried Second Mortgage

Besides using seller financing, assuming a mortgage is probably the most cost-effective way to own the property with little or no cost for a loan. One way you can use seller carried second mortgages is by you assuming the first mortgage and negotiating with the seller to take out a second mortgage for any equity in the property. As an added bonus to get the seller to help finance you, you can agree to pay an extra amount of interest above what the seller may be paying on the first mortgage; this is like an added bonus to the seller for financing you.

Financing a deal is all about creating a win-win for all parties; this is where the creative part of creative financing comes into play. Another way you can use seller carried second mortgage financing is if you cannot come up with all the cash, but you still want to go through with the purchase. For instance, let us say that the price for the property you are interested in costs $300,000. In this case you are only able to come up with $250,000 from financing and just cannot come up with the rest. You could simply ask the seller to accept a note for the remaining $50,000 and still close the deal.

If you want a deal done bad enough, you will sometimes have to find a way to make it happen. There are many books dedicated to creative strategies that people have used to structure deals; if you have ever heard of the saying "there's more than one way to skin a cat" then you know you have more than one way to do something, especially in real estate.

Traditional financing can be to way to go. But if your credit is not up to par then there is a multitude of other ways to go about seeking financing. You can explore an equity partner, home equity loans (HELOC), credit card line of credit, using the potential of the property, life insurance policy, IRA (there are rules to this so be careful), your family members, and so on.

Look into these and other viable options, find what works for you, and get your hustle on. For the record, single family homes offer a wider range of financing options than other forms of real estate. For me, I love the opportunities present in multifamily apartments and mixed-use buildings; dream big and you will win big as I like to believe, but you have to do what is right for your goals.

I know this may seem like a lot of information to take in and I know you may be nervous. I was and at times I still am, however, Teddy Roosevelt said it best when he stated, “The only man [woman] who never makes a mistake is the one who never does anything.” However, in finance, as I mentioned in the introduction, if you never do anything you have already failed – that too is a mistake.

So far, we have looked at real estate as an investment, how to finance it, different types of properties, and factors that can affect it. Now I will explain a few ways that you can evaluate a property to see if you should purchase it or move on to another project.

EVALUATING REAL ESTATE

When it comes to evaluating a property, it can be done in one of three ways: sale comparison, cost approach, or income approach. I will discuss each type, but for the purpose of this section I will mainly focus on the income approach, since we are looking to purchase income-producing properties. These different approaches help take the emotional appeal of investing out as well as having the previous owner's purchase price determine the value of the property. By using these methods, you can discover the true value of the property based on facts and numbers.

Sales Comparison Approach

This is probably the easiest method to learn and is the most commonly used when buying single family residences. With this method you are simply comparing one property to another through the substitution process. What that means is that you are adding and subtracting value based on recent sales of properties that are similar to the property you are investigating; this is known as a comparable or a "comp" in industry terms.

Most sources on the Internet offer this service if you are looking for properties on sites such as Trulia, Realtor.com, or Loopnet.com. You can get a good feeling for the value of property by checking the market based on comps. Other sources for finding comps include Realtor publications, brokers, appraisers, and public records. This method is very reliable if good sales comps exist.

When using sales comps, you want to look at a minimum of three comparable properties that are similar to your property of interest. There will be some differences between the properties such as size, number of bedrooms, age and so on. This is where you have to take the price the comp sold for and make adjustments up or down to make it look like the property of interest.

Adjustments can be made based on characteristics such as overall condition, age of home, garage, bedrooms, bathrooms, or square footage. For instance, let us assume that you are looking to buy a three-bedroom house as your property. There is a two bedroom home five blocks away that sold for $150,000 six weeks ago. In this area a three bedroom goes for $5,500 more than a two bedroom, so you add the value to the comp to make it worth the same price as your property of interest. In this example, you could reasonably expect a three-bedroom home to go for $155,000 based on this sales comp. After taking your comps and performing your analysis, you should make the necessary adjustments and figure out the probable value for your property of interest.

Cost Approach

The cost approach is an appraisal based on the assumption that the structure needs replacement. One definition describes it as "the land value, plus the cost to reconstruct any improvements, less the depreciation on those improvements." Think of this as a similar approach to what is used by the insurance companies when your car is damaged or totaled and the adjuster has to come out and do an appraisal. For the cost approach, you have two costs that need to be weighed: *reproductions cost* versus *replacement cost*.

Reproductions cost is the cost of building the same structure in the same manner while replacement cost is the cost of replacing the structure with modern material and current standards of design; this tends to set the limit on the current value. This type of approach is typically reserved for commercial type building or newer structures where there are no comparable properties. Think about the Notre Dame Cathedral being repaired due to the fire damage, and this is the type of cost that is similar in nature.

When it comes to the replacement method the problem is that the amount of depreciation that is accrued can be difficult to determine, which makes this a judgment call based on the property conditions, and we all know what happens when judgment and feelings get involved. This is why the focus for real estate will be the income approach, which deals with logic and reasoning not emotional attachment or pro forma projection.

Income Approach

This approach attempts to measure the property value by converting expected future income into a lump sum amount on an annualized base, or for a twelve-month period.

Investors who are looking to rent their property to others mainly use the income approach to determine the value of the property. There are several things you should know in order to estimate the value of a property using this method. The formula for income property valuation begins with an estimation of income and expenses; the whole formula looks like this:

Potential Gross Income/Gross Scheduled Income

- Minus: Vacancy and Collection Loss Allowance (V/C)
- Equals: Effective Gross Income (EGI)
- Minus: Operating Expenses (maintenance, utilities, etc.)
- Equals: Net Operating Income (NOI)
- Minus: Debt Services (mortgage, if any)
- Equals: Cash Flow Before Taxes (CFBT)

The potential gross income, or gross scheduled income, describes the rent that is collectable if every single unit is fully occupied for the year. This takes into account 100 percent of the building and gives you the best-case scenario. From the potential gross income, you subtract any vacancy and collection losses. This portion of the formula takes into account any uncollected or lost rent as well as income you are losing because units are not rented and bad debts by tenants. You can calculate these losses based on the rate of other local ownership and management or create a chart based on the "actuals" if you can get the information from the current owner.

Actuals are all pertinent information about the property. This includes rent roll, which shows what units are filled and the amount of rent being paid; it can also include the properties income statement, statement of cash flows, as well as maintenance logs for the property. This information will allow you to review how the property is being run and can help you make an accurate bid based on factual information.

To continue, miscellaneous income was not included in this formula but should be if the property is receiving additional income from amenities, such as storage fees, vending machines, laundry room services, or parking fees. You would add this in to get an accurate picture of your expected gross income (EGI) for the property. Knowing this portion is a major step in helping you get to your bottom line or cash flow.

Once you have the EGI, you will need to subtract any operating expenses associated with running the property. These expenses can include items such as insurance, property management fees, property taxes, supplies, repairs, maintenance, etc. Operating expenses will deal with the operation of the business or the day-to-day dealings to make the property run smoothly and excludes any debt services or mortgage payments; it is the overhead associated with the property, including fixed and variable expenses.

Once this is subtracted from the EGI, you are left with your net operating income (NOI). The NOI is your income before accounting for income taxes, interest, and principal payments. After getting the NOI, you need to subtract your mortgage payments. As I mentioned earlier, this valuation is on an annualized base, so if a mortgage payment was $500 a month it should appear as $6,000 when you are compiling your data. Once you have subtracted the debt service from the NOI, you are left with your cash flow before taxes (CFBT).

I know that this may all sound confusing, so I will give an illustration to better help convey the information. Imagine that you are about to purchase a 40-unit apartment building for $1,000,000 and you expect to make a $200,000 down payment. The unit mix for this apartment includes 25 units that rent for $400 a month and 15 that rent for $525 a month. The vacancy and collection loss for this particular area is 5 percent and you have no other income coming in from this property.

The operating expenses total 25 percent of the gross income, and based on the remaining balance of $800,000, which you acquired as a back loan, you have an annual debt service of $75,916.20. Also, as a reserve, you plan to set aside $10,700 a year for any unexpected maintenance. With all this information, what is your cash flow before taxes?

Based on the formula mentioned earlier, the first thing you have to do is to figure out what is the potential gross income for the property on an annualized basis. This can be done by multiplying the number of units by the monthly rent and then times that by twelve. For this example, the potential gross income total is $214,500. You can see this based on the information below:

Gross Potential Income: 25 (units) x $400 x 12 = $120,000
15 (units) x $525 x 12 = $94,500
Total: $214,500

Next, you have to figure out the vacancy and collections loss allowance. According to the example the estimate is 5 percent, so in order to get the dollar amount you must convert this to a decimal and multiple it by the potential gross income. This will give you a V/C allowance of $10,725.

V/C allowance: $214,500 x .05 = $10,725

After subtracting the V/C allowance from the gross potential income, you end up with your effective gross income, which totals

$203,775 since the property has no other income. The nest step in the formula is to subtract operating expense for the EGI so that you are one step closer to getting to the cash flow before taxes on your property.

Operating expenses are 25 percent of EGI, so as we did with the V/C allowances, you must do with the operating expenses. After subtracting operating expenses of $50,943.75, you have a net operating income of $152,831.25.

Operating Expenses: $203,775 x .25 = $50,943.75

Net Operating Income: $203,775 - $50,943.75 = $152,831.25

At this point you are almost done with your calculations; the only step left is to figure out the cash flow before taxes. To do this you subtract your debt service and reserve account from the NOI. By completing this step, you realize that the property has a cash flow before taxes of $66,215.05. Remember, the reserve account value totaled $10,700 and your annual debt service was $75,916.20.

Cash Flow before Taxes:

$152,831.25 - $10,700 - $75,916.20 = $66,215.05

This gives you an annual cash flow of $66,215.05 before having to give Uncle Sam a piece of the profits. CFBT are your profits left over after servicing the property and equates to about $5,517.92 per month that flows into your pockets. Once you have your CFBT, you can evaluate the property based on other factors such as cash-on-cash return (COC). To figure out the percentage for COC, you will use the following formula:

Cash-on-cash = CFBT ÷ Equity

Since we already know all known information for this formula all we have to do is plug and play. CFBT is equal to $66,215.05 and your equity is your down payment of $200,000. Once you enter the numbers, you realize that your COC is roughly 33 percent.

Your COC return allows you to determine your expected return in the first year of ownership after using OPM. This is a quick read on the property, and it allows you to compare the return to other investments. This return is far superior to any other type of investment, such as a bond, certificate of deposit, or savings account. What other investment can potentially give you a 33 percent return on your money in the first year? There are few, if any at all, besides real estate.

The methods previously discussed are all ways that investors evaluate potential properties; however, the one method that was not mentioned in that group was the capitalization rate, or "cap rate." The cap rate is used to help estimate the value of your income property; it measures the absolute return in dollars invested if you were to pay all cash for the investment property without the use of leverage. The formula for finding the cap rate is:

Cap rate = NOI ÷ Value of property

If you were to use the previous example of the 40-unit building that was valued at $1,000,000 and had an NOI of $152,831.25, you end up with a cap rate of 6.54 percent. As you can see, paying for the property in all cash will give you a return that is slightly higher than inflation, however it would not be advantageous to do so when you can get a better return using leverage.

What I mean is, you will get a 33 percent return using $200,000 of your own funds with $800,000 as leverage versus 6.54 percent return using the whole $1,000,000 in cash, so why use all your own money? If you did have the full $1,000,000 to invest, then imagine that you are able to purchase a total of five properties valued at $1,000,000 each, with a down payment of $200,000 in equity on each property. This is called opportunity cost; it is when you compare the benefits of one thing to another. In this situation you could possibly have five income-producing properties with positive cash flow compared to just one that is fully amortized.

Finally, if you have evaluated the property and concluded that it makes economic sense, then you need to find out the debt service ratio to see if the property will pass the institutional test, if financed with leverage. Most institutions prefer a debt service ratio of 1.2 or higher. This means that the property produces 20 percent more net income than needed to make its mortgage payments. To find the debt service ratio (DSCR) you would use the following formula:

Debt service = NOI ÷ Annual mortgage payment

Using the same example, we find the DSCR for the 40-unit building to be 2.01, which means that the property exceeds the minimum requirements; your property can pay the mortgage twice over. Once you have completed your analysis, your income statement for the property should look like this:

Property 1
Income Statement

Gross Potential Income:

25 units @ $400/mo.	$120,000
15 units @ $525/mo.	$94,500
	$214,500

Less: Vacancy/Collection Loss	($10,725.00)
Equals: Effective Gross Income	$203,775.00
Less: Operating Expenses @ 25	($50,943.25)
Equals: Net Operating Income	$152,831.25
Less: Debt Service	($75,916.25)
Reserve Account	($10,700.00)
Equals: Cash Flow before Taxes	$66,215.05

Cash-on-cash:	33.1%
Cap rate:	6.54%
Debt service:	2.01

Based on this information and other key pieces that you have utilized, you will then decide if this property makes sense for you. This is only an example; expenses will most likely be higher than 25 percent of EGI, unless there is some major deferred maintenance, or everything is handled by the owner.

Other than that, the property can handle itself in regard to mortgage payments, which can be covered twice over. Also, your COC is high at roughly 33 percent. Based on this information, your payback period is less than four years so you will recoup your initial investment and start to earn infinite returns on your money, because you will essentially have no money of your own involved.

There is more to real estate than what is in this short chapter, and it may seem like a lot of information still, but it is so much simpler once you take action and start doing it. It is no different than seeing an instruction manual that seems like it is a mile long only to find out that once you have read it and taken action, it really is not that difficult to follow. This can go for improving your credit, investing, trading, or real estate.

You will not be perfect in getting any of this right because things will happen, but if you keep an open and logical mind you will win more often than you lose. Even if the methods I have discussed in this chapter, or in the book overall, are not for you or you create your own along the way, the overall goal of this book is to help you identify ways to become financially successful in your own right. Whatever methods you employ, you should utilize them to the fullest.

With that being said, the next chapter will focus on how you can protect your assets, pass them on, and stay financially successful without losing everything should litigation, unfortunate circumstances, or even death arise.

5

ASSET PROTECTION

If you employ everything for the proceeding chapters perfectly, it will all mean nothing without protecting your assets. Passing on your fortune to your children, charitable giving, and self-protection are all fundamental considerations that can be accomplished by various means: trusts, legally structured businesses, insurance, and wills.

The structure you employ to protect your assets will depend on your situation, and you should consult an accountant and an attorney on how to best to accomplish your goals. In this chapter I will discuss several means of asset protection, the benefits of using these methods, and how they work. I am not a professional and the information contained herein is only for information purposes, as the laws can change rapidly. I strongly encourage you to seek professional advice when it comes to the following legal instruments.

WILLS

Almost everyone has heard of a will, or a "last will and testament." A will is simply a written document explaining how your assets will be distributed once you have passed away. Even though a will is not necessarily the best way to go about protecting your assets, it should still be considered.

The reason a will is not one of the best methods for planning is because the will has to go through probate, and this is something that you want to avoid if you have significant assets. Probate is defined as "the procedure by which a transaction alleged to be a will is judicially established as a testamentary disposition and also applies to the administration process of an estate." Basically, this means that the courts will be involved in the division of your assets, which can be costly, and almost anyone can contest your will.

You should not want to bicker over your assets once you are gone, and with proper planning both bickering and probate can be avoided. If you want an example of inefficient planning, then look at Aretha Franklin's situation with her family and how she did not leave a legitimate will.

Though wills are not the best tool for asset protection, they are necessary in some cases, like designating a guardian for minor children or transferring property to a trust that was not transferred before your demise.

There are some things that will be required to make your will a legal document. You will need witnesses, an executor representative, you will have to be of legal age, and the document will have to be typed or printed, among other requirements. It is best to have your will drafted by a lawyer and you should allow him or her to maintain possession of it for safekeeping after it is prepared. It is also important to note that laws vary from state to state, so confirm the status of your will if you decide to move or change states.

To create a valid and legal will, the law requires that you know the nature and extent of your property, know who will inherit your estate in case there is no will, and understand the distribution plan you have created. Upon completion of a legal will, you will be known as the testatrix (if you are female) or testator (if you are male) of the will; this fulfills the testamentary capacity required for creating a legal will.

As for witnesses, check the technical requirements of your state. Most states have similar rules such as witnesses must see you sign and then sign afterwards, or the witnesses should be in the same room and use the same pen to initial or sign the necessary documents.

Drafting a will can come in various forms, so check with your state as to what type of will is allowed. These forms can include, but are not limited to a holographic will, oral will, statutory will, joint will, or video will. With a holographic will, the whole document is written and signed by the testatrix or testator; no witnesses are required. The downfall to this type of will is that the document can be forged. Once again, check with your local state to see if this particular type is available for use.

An oral will is usually accepted under special circumstances such as imminent death. Last I checked, only a few states allow this type of will and some only allow it for members of the armed forces before death, and only then where property is limited. For example, I was in the U.S. Army and deployed to both Iraq and Afghanistan. Suppose I was hit by an improvised explosive device (IED) and there was no possibility of survival; I could give an oral will for the personal property with which I deployed.

States such as California and Michigan allow the use of statutory wills. A statutory will is where you can create a legally valid will on a printed form; it is simply a fill-in-the-blank sheet. I am no legal expert and many of you probably are not either, but logically this could end up doing more harm than good. Saving a few dollars on the front end could end up costing you and your recipients on the back end.

A joint will is self-defined; it is where two people create a will together. Usually these are for married couples and once one spouse dies the other survivor gets everything. This is not a guarantee, however. With this type of will certain contingency steps need to be taken.

Finally, we come to video wills. With the way people record just about everything, this may soon be the preferred method to draft a will. Technology has revolutionized a lot of things and asset protection is no different. This type of will can be beneficial in cases where memory has faded or if the person is facing imminent danger, like being trapped in a mass shooting situation. On the other hand, the downside to video wills is that the video can be altered, but not as easily as a written document.

With all the various types, you can get so involved in the creation of your will that you forget things that could affect it: marriage, divorce, or children born after the creation of said will. Marriage can range from getting married after the execution of a will to getting a divorce and remarrying someone else. You should note that a large portion of states have laws that award the spouse a share of your assets, called intestate share, unless it appears in your will that he or she was intentionally left out. So, ensure that you revise or make supplements to your will accordingly.

In some states a divorce will void all provisions to that spouse so you may not have to worry about making revisions; however, check with your state laws in regard to specifics on wills. Some states will treat the former spouse as if he or she died before you, so as to protect any children in the plan, while in other states the transfer of any assets to the former spouse is null and void. The only exception to this is with a life insurance policy; in this case the spouse who is the named beneficiary will receive compensation according to contractual law. So, if you do not want that ex to get that check, then ensure your records are up to date.

With all this talk of marriage and divorce there may be children involved. Children come along and change everything from your daily routine to your sex life, and even your will; therefore, it is wise to revise your will to reflect these necessary changes. In any case, most states have statutes providing for any children born after the execution of the original will.

Even with all the precautionary measures, the aforementioned may not cover all your property. Therefore, it is extremely important to include a residuary clause within your will. This clause will provide for the distribution of the remainder of your estate after all the specifics and cash bequests have been made. It is really a blanket contingency clause, or a "cover your ass" (CYA) clause, in case any other contingency or bequest you have made fails. Any bequest that fails, for whatever reasons, automatically reverts back to the estate.

Even though wills are not necessarily the best tool to use alone, it should be part of your asset protection plan. I am sure you would not want you hard-earned wealth to end up with the wrong person or have Uncle Sam benefit from all the time dedicated to your acquisitions. Next, I will discuss something that you can create to strengthen your will, and this wonderful instrument is called a trust.

TRUST

Trusts are the most flexible devices available when it comes to estate planning and asset protection and should be considered in everyone's plan. It can be revocable or irrevocable, or created during your lifetime (inter vivos) or upon death (testamentary).

Trusts can help satisfy different planning needs and they can be defined as a legal entity created to control the distribution of property.

Trusts are income-producing entities, much like corporations and LLCs, and can be used to avoid putting substantial amounts of income-producing property into the hands of a child or someone who is financially irresponsible; think of a trust fund baby. In the previous chapter we discussed purchasing rental property to produce income; well, a trust could be the answer to how you pass it on to family, friends, or charity.

This form of asset protection can get complicated, so seek competent legal advice. Earlier in this book I mentioned how the wealthy have ways to avoid taxes or defer them legally, this is one of the ways it can be done. A trust can allow you to avoid, defer, or decrease your income and transfer taxes as well as provide control over minors or dependents through distribution.

A trust will consist of certain components such as the grantor, the trustee, and the beneficiary. The grantor is simply the person who creates the trust and decides what property will be transferred to the trust, who the trustee is, and how the funds may be utilized; this is by no means an exhaustive list explaining the capacity of the grantor, it is simply basic starter information.

The trustee is appointed by the grantor and is entitled to a commission or fee for services but does not receive any benefits from the trust itself unless this person is a named beneficiary. As a trustee, this person is the owner of the legal title property in the trust; this makes the trustee responsible for the management of the trust assets as well as keeping them separate and accounted for. If you do not appoint a successor trustee, the court will be more than happy to name one for you. The whole point of having this setup is to keep outsiders, like the court system, out of your business, so please ensure your bases are covered.

A qualified lawyer can help you out in this aspect. As far as naming a trustee goes, this person must be qualified to handle all financial, accounting, and management duties necessary to administer the property of the trust. The last component of a trust is the beneficiary. The beneficiary is the individual or group of individuals receiving the primary benefit from the trust property, making the primary beneficiary entitled to any income the trust may earn: Other individuals or organizations, known as remainder beneficiaries, are entitled to the principal after the entitlements to the primary end.

Irrevocable Trusts

An irrevocable trust is one that cannot be revoked or amended by the grantor. One reason to create this type of trust is for the purpose of reducing the potential transfer taxes on the property by removing it from your estate. An irrevocable trust removes the rights of the grantor to amend, revoke, or alter the trust in any way. It also removes your ability to control ownership enjoyment of the property or income generated by the property, so think twice before acting.

Inter Vivo Trust

An inter vivo trust can be revocable or irrevocable and is made while the grantor is still alive. A trust of this kind can be made in one of two ways: 1) the grantor can declare the holding of personal property for the benefit of another, or 2) the grantor can transfer title to a trustee for the benefit of his or herself, another person, or a group of people.

The first way in which to create an inter vivo trust is known as a declaration of trust; this is where the grantor becomes the trustee. This could be an issue and raise questions regarding the validity of the trust. This will happen when the grantor serves as the trustee and sole beneficiary of the trust and no valid trust intent can be found.

One reason that a person may create a trust in this manner is to take advantage of the tax benefits of an inter vivo trust; it allows you to shift income from one person to another. The validity of your trust will not be questioned as long as there is an interest created for the beneficiary other than the grantor, this will still be valid even if the grantor decides to retain extensive power over the trust.

Testamentary Trust

A testamentary trust is one that is created in accordance to your will and only takes effect after your death. Most of the time testamentary trusts are used when a person does not want to part with a certain property during his or her lifetime but wants the control that a trust can provide. It is important for you to know that a trust of this kind will not result in any immediate estate or income tax savings but may do so when the will is executed.

Trusts come in various forms and can be used for just about anything. If you are like me and have children you would like to pass on your wealth to, then you should look into creating a dynasty trust. This is another form that wealthy individuals use to continuously create generational wealth for their families long after the grantor has passed. When you transfer property to a trust and take advantage of the unified credit and generational-skipping tax exemption, you and your descendants could defer payments of any transfer tax on property for a century or more!

The great thing about a dynasty trust is that it allows you to create life income interests in successive generations; And you do not have to worry if you are currently married or on the brink of divorce because a dynasty trust will protect the beneficiary's assets from being taken in a divorce proceeding or against any creditors.

As I have said before, I am by no means a lawyer or legal expert; I am merely relaying the information as I comprehend it, so please consult a legal representative on the steps necessary to protect and pass on your assets. Next, we will be discussing the use of insurance as a way to help protect your assets and loved one.

INSURANCE

Life insurance is something that cannot be emphasized enough when it comes to planning your estate. In some cases, this may be a person's largest asset. Having life insurance helps you improve your planning for the family and develops its optimum value at the time of your death.

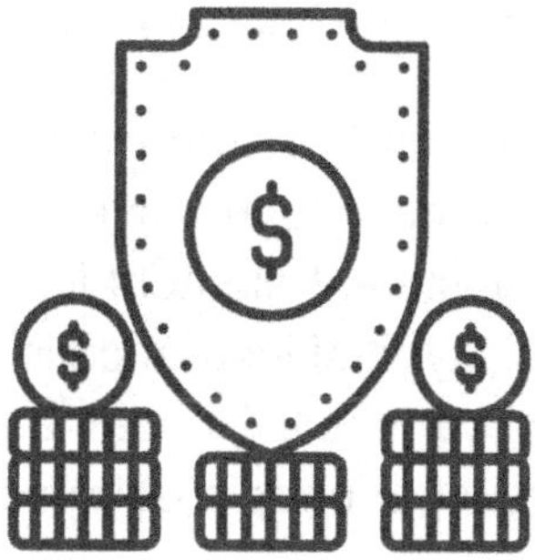

Trillions of dollars in estates are waiting to be passed on to the next generation. This is good and bad. Good, in the sense that someone has made plans to keep their family going after death. Bad, because of the potential transfer tax rates and any death taxes that may be applied by the state. These alone will eat away at the wealth you would like to leave behind.

This is where sufficient life insurance coverage can be helpful to your financial, asset protection, or estate plan. There are many reasons for acquiring life insurance. Some are: 1) the ability to provide liquidity to satisfy transfer taxes, 2) you create assets in an estate, 3) you can shelter assets against transfer tax and minimize the transfer of property, and 4) insurance allows you to replace income that is lost by your death if you are the primary money maker. The last stated reason for insurance is known as key person insurance (KPI).

Insurance can offer some favored tax advantages and any borrowing against the policy is usually favorable and tax free, which can allow you to purchase assets such as real estate (see chapter four: creative financing).

As far as potential transfer tax goes, you can create what is known as a "life insurance trust" that will pass on the insurance proceeds free of the transfer tax to beneficiaries. Consult with a legal expert for the ins and outs of this type of trust.

You have your pick of the litter when it comes to choosing different types of insurance policies. The types of policies include term, whole life, variable life, universal life, and annuities, to name a few.

With term insurance you get the advantage of low costs. Term insurance can have many variations and is not based on an investment element like other forms of insurance. The setback to this type of insurance is that as you get older it costs more for you to be insured under this policy. Term insurance is typically for younger people or someone needing coverage short term.

Whole life is one of the insurance concepts with an investment element to it. With whole life insurance your death benefits are fixed, as well as the maturity date, premiums, and the progression of the cash value. Another advantage of the policy is that it allows you to borrow against the cash value for emergencies, to payoff credit card debt, or for investing purposes, such as real estate.

Many people have borrowed against their policies in order to fund or start a business, pay for a child's college, or for their child's wedding; it is like a supercharged savings account. The buildup of cash can be looked at as a forced saving plan for those of us who cannot seem to save. I must advise you that there are some financial "experts" who advocate not purchasing a whole life insurance policy when it comes to cash value, so do adequate research on your own before deciding to make a decision of this magnitude.

Variable life insurance is a variation of whole life that allows flexibility in the choice of investment vehicles. You can invest your net premiums in a fund or funds of your own choosing. The downside to that is that if the markets fall it will have a severe effect on your policy. On the other hand, if the fund you choose earns more than a specified return, then your death benefit and cash value will increase. However, if the fund earns less, your benefit does not depreciate below the face value.

This policy is no different than what you may have learned in chapter two on investing, so if you know what you are doing and have done adequate research, then this type of policy can essentially be another form of a defined contribution plan for you.

Universal life insurance is a popular insurance product that combines the features of a whole life plan and a term insurance plan. This plan allows for flexibility in the face value and premium payments. With universal life, part of the premiums is invested in a cash fund that is then invested in fixed income assets (read: bonds). The other portion of the premiums is used to finance renewable term insurance.

You can increase or decrease the amount of the death benefit as well because of your ability to vary the premium payments. Check with your insurer on the specifics of this type of policy because you could end up with some tax liabilities if this type of policy fails to meet certain requirements.

Annuities are nothing more than a structured payment program. Under this form, your beneficiary receives installments instead of a large lump sum. You can basically do the same thing under a trust and the trust will more than likely be cheaper. Plus, a trust would allow you more flexibility.

So far, we have discussed trusts, wills, and insurance as ways to help protect your family and assets; next we will delve into corporate structures.

LEGAL STRUCTURES

I saved this form of asset protection last for multiple reasons. One, if you plan properly then your assets can be protected from claims against third parties. Two, the devices that I will mention can afford you better protection that is above the previously mention insurance plans. And three, I just thought it fitting to end the chapter on this topic.

The two corporate structures that will be covered in this section are limited liability company (LLC) and the family limited partnership (FLP). Just for general education, I will also introduce you to other business structures that may or may not offer the best protection; this will include sole proprietorship, general and limited partnerships, and corporations.

Asset Protection

Limit Liability Company (LLC)

This wonderful little entity offers the same limited liability as a corporation but may be taxed as a partnership or corporation. In all actuality, it is a hybrid partnership-corporate entity. This organizational form comes from the need and desire for a structure that is taxed as a partnership yet protects its owners from unlimited liability.

This business structure is fairly new, with the first LLC being enacted in 1977, in Wyoming. Roughly forty states have approved this business entity with

Wyoming and Nevada (Las Vegas) being the most favorable states towards limited liability companies.

A limited liability company, under most definitions, is an unincorporated structure with two or more members formed under state law. This definition fails to mention that you are able to create a one-person or one-member LLC as well.

Creating an LLC is as simple as filling out the appropriate paperwork, in this case an article of organization, and filing it with your appropriate state agency. An article of organization will state the name of the business or entity, the date it was created, names or any managers, and the nature of the business. The LLC should also have an operating agreement describing the interest of each member regarding any capital, profits, and liabilities. This is important if there is more than one member with ownership interest.

Any owners in the LLC are referred to as members, and all members are responsible for the management of the LLC unless otherwise specified in the operating agreement. Members are issued a certificate that shows their percentage of ownership. Typically, the founding owners of the LLC will designate how many memberships certificates the LLC will issue.

Creating an LLC has many advantages. It provides protection of assets, absence of personal liability, shelter from double taxation, flexibility in management and organization, and allows for foreign investors in the company. It also allows you to outsource to someone who will file your paperwork and keep minutes for any meetings, which means that you have one less thing to worry about.

This business form is not without its disadvantages, however. This can include the inability to issue stock, and an LLC may be limited to a certain lifespan, such as 30 years.

Family Limited Partnership (FLP)

A family limited partnership is said to be a legal entity that can provide asset protection and allows for management and control of assets. For many wealthy families this has been, or at least can be, a cornerstone for the transfer of wealth. An FLP allows you to do business in a partnership form and limits your liability, much like an LLC. If you decided you wanted to use an FLP, you would contribute property to a limited partnership in exchange for general and limited partnership interests. Afterwards, you could gift limited partnerships to family members or a trust for their benefit while you maintain the general partnership.

This in effect allows you to clear the property out of your personal estate, which can reduce taxes and could allow you and your family to take advantage of the generational-skipping transfer tax exemption. A generational-skipping tax is one that is imposed on you by the government to prevent you from passing on property to two or more generations below you without paying a transfer tax.

You know Uncle Sam has to try and get his piece of the pie. At the time of this writing the rate for the transfer tax is between 35-40 percent of the property value that is transferred. Also, each individual that you gift to has up to $5,000,000 that can be exempt from the transfer tax.

This is why an FLP can be advantageous to have. Along with the potential to prevent high taxes that diminished your family wealth, an FLP has other benefits too. It can shelter the gift from creditors of any recipient. Among other things, there is a reduced asset value (between 10-50 percent) for transfer tax purposes through discount valuations and you can maintain control of the assets while remaining the general partner and still make substantial gifts.

You can get the most advantage from an FLP by transferring property that will appreciate in value, like real estate or securities. This can be even better if you use a combination of an FLP and an asset protection trust. This can be achieved by transferring one or more gifts to the trust of a limited partner's interest (your family member). Overall, you can easily protect and pass on your assets if you utilize the proper entities. I recommend consulting with an attorney as to how best accomplish this. Next, we will discuss some good and not so good ways to structure your entity.

Other Forms of Organizing

Sole Proprietorship

This business organization is one owned by a single individual who is entitled to all the profits of the business and is also responsible for all the business debt. There is no separation between the two and this form of organization can fall under "doing business as" or DBA if you are using a name other than your own for a business. This form can have its advantages and is often used in the beginning stages of a business.

Advantages of a sole proprietorship includes profits going straight to the owner, there is no special taxation, it is easy and inexpensive to form, and you have direct control of the business, unlike forms such as a corporation. These may all sound fine and dandy, but the end goal should be asset protection and this form will not suffice for extended periods of time. This is due to several disadvantages, such as you being responsible for all debt, which exposes you to unlimited liability.

This means that if you are sued under this business form and you do not have enough insurance coverage or cash on hand to cover debts, then you could lose your business as well as your personal assets, such as your home. Also, it is hard to raise capital and it can take up a large portion of your time, time that you could be using to create more assets.

Partnerships

A partnership is an association that consists of two or more people coming together as co-workers for the purpose of owning and operating a business for profit. With this form, much like a sole proprietorship, there is no separation between the owners in regard to debt, profits, or being sued.

We are talking about a general and limited partnership here, unlike the family limited partnership (FLP) previously mentioned. This partnership is when you are taking on an outside business partner or partners who provide access to equity in return for ownership. The FLP is where you are gifting property to family members who became limited partners while you maintained general partnership.

In this form of a partnership now being discussed, the general partner would be the person running the business and would also be the one facing unlimited liability for any debt of the business, whereas the limited partner(s) are only liable up to the amount of equity invested in the business. This type of partnership does have its advantages though.

Partnerships of this kind are easy and inexpensive to form, like sole proprietorships; they allow for an unlimited number of partners or owners; and there is no special taxation. On the flip side of that, you have to look at the disadvantages of this form, which can include having to share profits, having difficulty in transferring ownership, and possible conflicts between partners that could lead to the dissolution of the business. Be careful when deciding to start a business with outside partners or family members to whom you are not transferring assets.

Corporations

A corporation can be defined as a business entity that legally functions separate and apart from its owner. For legal purposes, a corporation can sue or be sued, and sell, purchase, or own property.

This business structure, because of its separate legal status, has many advantages. 1) The owner's liability is limited to the amount invested in the company, much like a limited partnership. 2) The life of the business is not tied to the investors, so death or withdrawal of an investor does not dissolve the business. And 3) it is easy to raise capital with this structure for expansion or for other business purposes.

A corporation is owned legally by its shareholders or owners who elect what is known as its board of directors. These people are responsible for appointing management who determine policies and the overall direction of the business. Corporations can be a good way to protect yourself and your personal assets, but there are drawbacks to this structure, like double taxation.

Corporate profits may be taxed once at the corporate level and then again if the business issues a dividend to shareholders. Other drawbacks can include government restrictions and the fact that this structure can be costly and complex to form.

There are also variations in the form corporations take. A C-Corporation, or C-Corp, as we have discussed, is the legal structure that is subject to corporate income tax where the owners, or shareholders, are taxed separately from the entity. An S-Corporation on the other hand, allows you to avoid the double taxation of profit by passing any profit or loss through to the shareholders, like a partnership. This structure has a number of restrictions that have taken away its desirability and made LLC's more popular. If you would still like to create an S-Corp, then consult with a lawyer who can walk you through the process.

This concludes the chapter on asset protection. The next subject, and final chapter, is on surrounding yourself with likeminded people. This also is the last step in the CITRAS™ method of finance. Man is a social creature who needs to communicate and share with others in order to continuously grow and expand. Being alone or surrounding yourself with people who are not on your level may cause you to become closed minded, and that is not healthy or profitable stance. I do not want this to happen to you, so let us move on to the finale.

6

SURROUNDING YOURSELF WITH LIKEMINDED PEOPLE

I am somewhat of a quote junkie, and the one that I found that fits this chapter exclaims, "No man or woman is an island; nobody get to the highest peaks without the help of others." This is most befitting of this chapter because 1) we are social creatures and love to be around others, 2) opportunities are limitless when you involve other great minds, and 3) we love to show off our knowledge to others and feel accepted.

I believe that if you are the smartest person in the room, then you are in the wrong room. You should strive to surround yourself with those who are smarter than you are, especially in areas where you may have a weakness. Seek out those who have the specialized knowledge where you may be lacking.

Have you ever heard that "birds of a feather flock together?" This entire chapter is on that subject. I could have given this chapter a creative title or name like Napoleon Hill in his book *Think and Grow Rich*, but I wanted to keep this plain and simple. Surrounding yourself with likeminded people not only benefits you, it benefits those you are around, and those you may seek to serve (consumers/clients) if your goal is a business venture.

And please don't misunderstand "likeminded" either. What I mean are simply people who are in the same frame of mind as you, in regard to succeeding financially or in any aspect of your life. I do not mean you surround yourself with people who think exactly like you. That would defeat your purposes. Now that this is cleared up, let us get on with the subject. The various relationships that will be discussed in this chapter are mentors, groups, and teams.

MENTORS

According to the *Merriam-Webster Collegiate Dictionary*, a mentor is defined as "a trusted counselor or guide." This means that your mentor is much like a tutor who helps you with a subject or problem you may not understand or foresee.

For the past six years I have not had a physical mentor because I am incarcerated, however, I do realize the importance of having one, or many. Initially I thought being autodidactic made me better, but now I see that this was closed-minded thinking on my behalf.

I say this because a good mentor can cut your learning time in half. It takes roughly 10,000 hours of practice or repetition to become a master of a craft (roughly 7-10 years), but a mentor could reduce that to five years or less if you are humble enough to learn and submit to his or her authority. I am mostly still learning on my own, but my mentors come in the form of books, practice, and talking to others who are on the same road to wealth building as I am.

I am not saying that you should be a lackey or be submissive to whomever you decide to take on as a mentor. I am saying that a mentor will be there to provide you with a richer and deeper knowledge of whatever field you are studying. They can help you streamline the learning process instead of spending years on your own learning what they already know. This will help you avoid pitfalls and mistakes.

Life is too short to be spent on learning something through the school of hard knocks. Someone else already took the time to learn it for you, benefit from that. It does not matter if the mentor is a good one or a bad one: you can learn something from both if you keep an open mind.

The military taught me that you will learn more from a bad leader than you will a good one, because a bad leader will teach you everything that you should not do while the good leader will only enhance your leadership skills. That is why you should keep an open mind with mentors.

Initially my flawed thinking came from the desire to be "self-made," so that I could say that no one gave me a damn thing or helped me. It was a sense of pride, a sense of utilizing my talents to achieve my goals by myself that led me down my previous path of thinking. I realized that a mentor of some kind was needed after two years of studying and learning on my own.

It was a quote from Wolfgang von Goethe that sparked the sudden change in my thinking: "A man of talent is not born to be left by himself, but to devote himself to art and good masters who will make something of him." This led me to think of how I previously developed my talents, before incarceration, which was through the use of schoolteachers, coaches, books, and craftsmen, who were more experienced than I was. Therefore it's good to surround yourself with mentors.

I have had both good and bad experiences with mentors, but a good one can provide you many advantages. A mentor can observe you in the work environment and provide constructive criticism. He or she can share the "secrets" learned over the course of the person's career; and your thinking can become more aligned with the mentor, which can create a beautiful relationship. The way I look at it is that you get the equivalent of a MBA or PhD without paying for it in money, time, or wasted experience.

It was not until I started doing the things I had read about or discussed with other likeminded individuals that I realized I did not have to continually waste my funds or time. By sharing knowledge and resources, the people in my small circle eventually became mentors to each other. Most of the people who have served in a mentor capacity have all been people I met through the military and were either high ranking noncommissioned officers (NCOs) or commissioned officers who had experience in real estate, finance, or investing and trading securities.

Many great and successful people have had mentors to guide them at some point. Alexander the Great had Aristotle, Warren Buffet had Benjamin Graham, and Carl Jung had Sigmund Freud. Every one of the aforementioned names is pretty well known and successful in their own right. From my experience, a mentor will challenge you and train you to think on a higher level, which allows you to make connections between different forms of knowledge.

For example, if you were a real estate investor you could make a connection between the economy, trading, and the housing market. Back in chapter three I mentioned several things that were important to trading and how all the markets can connect by focusing on the economy, business, and the consumer. Interest rates are also a major connecting factor between the economy, trading, and real estate. If rates are low, then people tend to borrow more, which leads to spending and investing. Interest rates for housing loans are also lower, so more people will look to buy or refinance than they will to rent. All of this can be evidenced in previous chapters, so I will not continue to stress this information; now let us get back to the subject at hand.

When you take on a mentor it is best to have as much personal interaction as possible. With technology it is easy to FaceTime or interact virtually, but you may miss out on key elements if this is your form of interaction. Personal interaction allows you to meet face-to-face and pick up on subtle aspects and cues that you will not get through virtual interaction.

I learned this key piece of information through my workout partner. I had never worked out by lifting weights before prison. I was 6' 5" and weighed 189 pounds; I was a string bean. I started buying workout books and doing what they instructed me to do because I wanted to get bigger. Eventually I did get bigger and stronger. I got up to 240 pounds on my own, but soon realized that it was not good for my knees. I was not used to that weight, and I suffered in some ways.

I worked out for five years by myself before I found a guy who took me on and showed me how to properly lift weights. I am stronger now at 220 pounds than I was at 240 pounds, because I learned proper technique by seeing an example, having him explain the process, and learning tricks of the trade. That is why personal interaction is better in a mentoring relationship.

Even though mentors may project an aura of power and authority, they too have strengths and weaknesses. Good mentors will allow you to develop your own style; these are the types of mentors you will most likely turn into lifetime friends and allies. A mentor of this caliber allows you to leave when the time is right or help you when it is that time. I equate this type of mentor relationship to the way some birds raise their young. The mentor is like the parent who feeds the young, inexperienced chick. Once you have been properly feed and taught what you need to know, then the parent pushes you out of the nest so that you can fly on your own and move on.

On the other hand, you can have mentors who become so dependent on having you around that they want to control you and not allow you to branch off from them. These are the types of mentors you should avoid. A mentor-mentee relationship is not a marriage and should not be an unconditional relationship. Mentors are similar to steppingstones. In life you will have many that can help you reach whatever goals you have in mind.

A good mentor relationship is one whereby you have a back and forth dynamic. This type of relationship encourages communication on both sides instead of the mentor doing all the teaching and talking. This dynamic can also encourage creative thinking and the development of new styles out of the old ones. In a roundabout way, you and the mentor are teaching each other and encouraging each other to not be stagnant.

I experienced this firsthand in my youth with my stepfather. I was about eleven years of age, and he was teaching me some of the master moves in checkers. He has been playing for years and I swear that at times he lives by those books and their antiquated strategies.

One day he was teaching me this one game that two grandmasters had played. He taught me for like 15 minutes straight, so of course I played the losing hand. This happened until we went live, and I had to play the game from memory. During the game play I switched up one of the moves because I saw something that the original players may not have at the time. That changed the whole dynamic of the game, and I ended up taking four of his pieces along with gaining a king for myself. We continued to play, and of course I still lost, but he was shocked and excited by what I had done. This led to us creating a back and forth dynamic thereafter.

The foundation of the mentor relationship should not fall only on the mentor. A good student of the game should absorb the ideas of the mentor and build upon them as their own. Friedrich Nietzsche said it best when he stated that "one repays a teacher badly if one remains only a pupil." This statement brings to mind a perfect example of this dynamic.

I have a really good friend of mines named Wes whose mother has a mentor who is a billionaire. His mother is into real estate and within the last year she created a structured deal on her own that allowed her to close on a house by being creative. She transformed what she already knew into something that was beneficial for her and the client.

Needless to say, his mother is working on more deals and will soon reach millionaire status likely within the following year. To top it off, she has made this a family business and is mentoring her children and grandchildren on the subject of real estate investing. Now she is the mentor and has created her own little dynamic group, which is the next subject I will discuss.

GROUPS

A group, according to Webster's, is defined as any collection or assemblage of persons or things; a number of persons or things ranged or considered together as being related in some way. A group is different from a team, yet the two are sometimes used interchangeably.

A group, by my definition, is a collection of people who come together to accomplish a task, and once the task is completed the group usually disperses. A group can have nothing else in common but the need to accomplish the task at hand; a group could become a team, but this is not always the case or overall goal. Most of us are familiar with groups, whether it is a Facebook group, work group, or something as intimate as a group of friends.

An example of a group being just a group occurred while I was in the military. My group consisted of myself and five other individuals. I communicated to the group each week what needed to be done and the timeline in which to complete the task. We came together for this specific purpose, and once the task was completed, we rarely conversed on other matters. We were sociable with each other, but beyond work we had nothing much to do with one another or to share.

On the other hand, a group that can evolve into something more intimate happened when I started playing organized sports; it all began with football for me. Initially we were kids looking to play the game for fun but through practice, interaction, and socialization we evolved into a team. My teammates and I went to school together, socialized, and occasionally hung out with each other on the weekends, so that we could be in sync.

Groups are an important part of this chapter because you can glean or share ideas on certain things. Joining groups such as a Real Estate Investment Association (REIA), a chat group on trading, a trade organization, or a fraternal order like the Freemasons can help you gain a tremendous advantage and allow you to develop team members from the group. Groups allow you to network with other likeminded individuals and share resources that you may not have had or obtained if you were alone. You may even find a mentor from the group to help guide you.

Groups are extremely popular in the age of technology. They are useful for getting tips and tricks of the trade or achieving a goal that you could not accomplish alone. Groups do not always have to extend to business. One group in particular that I was a part of was on X-Box Live. My group was in relationship to the game *Call of Duty,* whereby we all played Zombie mode.

It was fun to play and learn the little tricks of the game to extend gameplay. My ex-wife and I played up to level 33 once, before being killed off by the zombie horde and hell hounds. Once we joined the group, we played up to level 86 before our Wi-Fi disconnect. So, as you can see, groups can serve a purpose in building your way to financial success or in your general life.

You should know the purpose of your group and how it operates so that you can gauge the usefulness of it. There are some groups that are individualistic in manner while others are for a common goal. Take the comic convention (Comic Con) for example. Its purpose is to bring together us nerds who share the love of comics, manga, anime, and all things fantasy and science fiction. Yet there is competition promoted through costumes and individual knowledge, where people flaunt their prowess.

You can also think of this in the trading world where groups of people are individually seeking profit from the market and each other based on speculation, information, and decision making from market chatter and research. A group of people coming together for one cause, such as decision making, can be evidenced in investment groups where individuals pool together money and make decisions about where the funds will be invested. These people are working together for a common cause, which is to make a profit. This group, if they decide to stay together, will eventually become a team with one person most likely controlling the funds, like a CEO. This person will still make the decisions based on all the other participants, but they will no longer be just a group. This leads us into our next section.

TEAMS

Webster's Dictionary defines a team as a number of persons associated in some joint action or number of persons forming one of the sides in a game or contest. A team is especially important if you plan to utilize real estate as one of your platforms to build financial success. Unlike a group, a team is all about synergy, whereby the parts are greater than the whole. What I mean is that typically in a *group* people can function separately or are responsible for one area of the project without concern for other areas, while in a *team* the effort is more like a body consisting of several parts to make the whole work. A team is ineffective if it is not in sync.

If you have ever played sports, you know that my last statement is true. Take football for instance. If the quarterback, offensive linemen, running backs, tight ends, and receivers are not on the same page, then the team will, more than likely, have a poor season. The tight end and receivers could end up running the wrong routes, which could lead to interceptions, incomplete passes, or turnover on downs. The O-line could miss blocks and tackle, which leads to the quarterback being sacked or a loss of yards. No matter how good your quarterback is, whether Aaron Rodgers or Tom Brady, if the team is not in sync they are bound to fail.

Teams and team members allow you to make up for any of your weaknesses, but only if you have the right mix of team members. Teams are an important part of CITRAS™, because once you get into real estate you will need a small team of people to help you manage and build wealth.

Even with investing and trading, you will need a team of sorts. With trading and investing you will need a broker, a brokerage firm, a tax accountant, and maybe a wealth manager if you get really good at either. When it comes to choosing a broker for your investing or trading team, you can choose either an individual or organization, like Merrill Lynch, Charles Schwab, or Fidelity. Brokers are useful because they act as an intermediary between you and the markets. You can check with the Securities and Exchange Commission (SEC) or the Financial Industry Regulatory Authority (FIRNA) to see if your broker is registered, has any negative reviews, or has any actions reported against them.

As far as choosing a brokerage firm goes, there are so many choices that you should select one based on the style of investing or trading you will be conducting. Your choice can include Robinhood, E*Trade, or any other player in the industry that allows trading and investing. A research of brokerage firms can also be conducted using FIRNA.

With this being your team, you are the captain or leader, and your members should be chosen based on your goals, therefore you need to conduct adequate research before choosing any old team member whether it is a broker or an accountant. In most cases, you will only get what you pay for.

When it comes to real estate investing, a team will consist of a much larger pool of personnel. Upon choosing members of your team, you should consider having a realtor or broker, a certified public accountant (CPA) with experience handling real estate investors, a maintenance team if you own multiple units, a lender or lenders, a title company, asset protection lawyer, and a lawyer experienced with evictions.

This is not an exhaustive list of the personnel for your team, but it is a good place to start if you want to stay in the game long term. A good realtor or broker can help you find some of the best offerings. Oftentimes you can get a new listing before it has a chance to hit the market, which gives you an advantage over another investor. This is commonly known as a pocket listing, whereby preferred investors on the realtor's list gets first dibs on a property before showcasing it to the broader market. You typically are offered these when the realtor knows your preferences or when you are known to purchase property in a timely manner, thereby saving the realtor time on advertising and promotions, which leads to a quick turnover that puts money in everyone's pocket.

It is important to cultivate a relationship with realtors and brokers especially in the area(s) you want to invest. More than likely they will be experts in that particular area and can provide valuable information.

A CPA who is experienced with real estate investors can be worth his or her weight in gold. This person should be familiar with most of the accounting laws regarding real estate taxes and liabilities and can save you thousands of dollars in taxes and restless nights.

A maintenance team is great to have because it will save you on repairs whenever necessary. This keeps you from having to hire a contractor for all the different problems that will arise. And it's good to have someone local who can cover other properties you own in their area. You could also use your maintenance team to fix and flip properties as an added bonus.

Being a team leader, you will sometimes have to think outside the box to keep people gainfully employed, or as the military calls it conducting "hip pocket training."

One member of your team that I initially failed to mention is a property manager. If you decide to hire a management team, the property management company will most likely have its own crew. Either way, this can be money well spent with the right management team.

A good lender is like a good friend in a time of need, especially when you want to close quickly on a property. Once you are an established investor and have built a good relationship with your bank, it becomes easier to get funds for your projects. It may even get to the point where your loan applications are fast tracked and you can close within 48-72 hours, with the way technology is moving.

I encourage you to have multiple lenders you can go to; you do not want to become too dependent on one lender for all your real estate needs. Having multiple lenders is like having different credit cards that you can use for various needs. For example, a small community bank could be used to fund local fix and flip properties or residential units while a major financial institution, such as Wells Fargo, could be used to finance commercial property. Having various lenders that you can choose between will keep you from burning through your sources, and it will keep them each happy as you do good business with them.

Having a title company on hand will come in handy throughout the closing process. First, the company will be useful in performing a title search on the property. They can also help you with title insurance, which will protect you against ownership claims. Title insurance will also guarantee that the title is free and clear of any liens or claims, that the seller is the owner of the property, and that the title owner has the right to sell or transfer property to someone else.

Secondly, a title company can provide valuable information on comps, foreclosures, and title holders so that you can structure a plan for purchasing any property. A good title company will be able to save you a lot of valuable time.

Last, but not least, the title company can help hold funds in an escrow account and ensure that documents are passed along to the appropriate parties with the distribution of any necessary funds. You should keep a good title company on your team, because you never know when you may find a great deal and need to close as quickly as possible.

The law is a complicated subject and too numerous in pages and legal jargon for just any one person to understand, more so when dealing with real estate. This is where having an attorney who specializes in the area of real estate can come in handy. You want to employ attorneys who have experience in this arena, whether it is in asset protection, rental agreements, or the process of eviction.

If you have no other members on your team, then you definitely want to hire a good attorney with real estate experience. I like how Robert Kiyosaki likened a good attorney to a quarterback and how he or she can take responsibility for coordinating your entire team.

When choosing an attorney, you should look for someone who has experience in various forms of real estate, has various support systems or networks, and is available to do the work you require of him or her. You can check with the American Bar Association to find attorneys in your locale and perform a due diligence check on that person, such as seeing if there are malpractice claims or complaints.

As I have said before, this is not a complete list of the team members you should employ on your roster. Depending on how big you intend to be, you should think about adding general contractors, architects, and engineers if you would like to develop properties. The possibilities are endless once you understand the power of teamwork.

Well folks, this concludes all the steps in CITRAS™, but I will not leave you three-quarters of the way full. I believe a good book will give you resources that will help lead you through its intended process, so on the following pages you can view several useful resources on the various chapters. Thank you for purchasing my book, and may you live long and prosper, until next time.

RESOURCE GUIDE

Before I proceed to give you the following resources, I want to reiterate that I am by no means an expert on the subjects presented in this book; I have only presented the information as I comprehend it and relayed any experience that I may have had on each subject. Each subject presented is based on my knowledge and research. For some of you it may very well work in the same manner as it has for my associates and me. However, I encourage you to do the work yourself and not take everything contained in this book as gospel; things are constantly changing in the finance, even as some of the resources below may have. Websites are especially prone to come and go, and some may not even exist by the time this hits the press. Nevertheless, these are the resources I recommend at this time:

BOOKS:

- The Richest Man in Babylon by George S. Clason
- *Currency Kings* by Ben Robson
- *How to Invest in Debt* by Michael Pellegrino
- The Everything Guide to Day Trading by David Borman
- Personal Finance at Your Fingertips by Ken Little
- The Affluent Investor by Dr. Phil DeMuth
- The Debt Escape Plan by Beverly Harzog
- The 17 Indisputable Laws of Teamwork by John C. Maxwell
- Real Estate Investing from A to Z by William H. Pivar
- The Game of Life and How to Play It by Florence Scovel Shinn
- ** Anything by Robert Kiyosaki**
- What Every Real Estate Investor Needs to Know About Cash Flow by Frank Gallineli

INTERNET SOURCES, MAGAZINES, PUBLICATIONS

- Business Wire
- The Wall Street Journal
- Investor Business Weekly
- thinkrealty.com
- realwealthnetwork.com
- ftc.gov
- myfico.com
- bankrate.com
- federalreserve.gov
- Center for Creative Leadership at: CCL.org
- loopnet.com
- lendingtimes.com
- census.gov
- factfinder.census.gov
- realtor.com

Made in United States
North Haven, CT
10 November 2026

22091364R00088